Dedicated to:

_____

_____

_____

_____

_____

I0099891

To: _____

From: _____

Date: _____

JVH
PUBLICATIONS

A close look at the
breakdown of society

BE FREE

from

RESENTMENT

josé & lidia zapico
P.H.D.'s

jva

Our Vision

To reach the nations by bringing them the authenticity of the Word of God; to build up the faith and knowledge of those who fervently desire that revelation through books, audio and video materials.

© First Edition 2010 (*English edition*)
ISBN: 1-59900-057-1

© Jose and Lidia Zapico. All rights reserved. No part of this publication may be reproduced, stored in a retrieval system, or transmitted in any form or by any means without the prior written permission of the authors.

Cover art designed by: Ximena Urra/Esteban Zapico
Interior design: Esteban Zapico

Bible Citations taken from The Holy Bible - New American Standard Bible

Images and illustrations: Images © 2010 Merkushev Vasiliy; Magicinfoto; Shadow216; Stasya555.
Used with permission from Shutterstock.com.
Gustave Dore Morte, Agag. Public domain.

Printed by: JVH Publications
www.jesusvivehoy.com

This book was originally published in Spanish under the title:
Se Libre del Rencor - Translation was provided by Ali Casielles
alialas5@hotmail.com

category: deliverance/Bible study/christian living

Table of Contents

Prologue

What is hate? If it isn't what a woman who is mistreated and battered by by an abusive husband, who at the same time ignores his own wounded soul after seeing his own father do the same thing to his mother, then what is hate? A young alcoholic male, succumbed to his wreckless environment of drugs and vices, who remembers the painful day when his parents abandoned him, leaving him to his own luck, may ask himself the same question; What is hate?

Medical doctors, psychiatrists, philosophers, theologians and statesman, all ask themselves the same question. Looking through hundreds of pages in academic books and journals, they look for reasons why human nature can not rid itself of its demonic torments. However, they can not find any definitive answers beyond the hurts and wounds of past cold, winer nights ….

Hatred is the opposite of love, but they come from the same source within the hearts of human beings. Each one of us has the capacity to choose whether to hate and keep the hidden grudges in our soul, or to love and forgive. Upon reading this marvelous book by José and Lidia Zapico, you will see how resentment has evolved across the ages, generation after generation. What once began as the hatred from one brother towards another from the beginning of creation, is today like a generational plague of evil and destruction capable of islating and destroying lives, families and entire nations. This book will show you not only an exact x-ray of what hatred is, how it is birthed within hearts and how it has extended across the lives of all oppressed by this evil. Additionally, how this monster has transformed from each successive generation, destroying lives, eliminating whole races, destroying ethnicities, stomping on belief systems and paralyzing through fear and intimidation.

Hatred has disrupted the lives of countless human beings through history, causing htem to have to run from one place to another from the fear of persecution by others who do not think like them.

It is interesting to note that mankind has atemptted to loose himself from his own fears without success. The number of persons tormented by fears of failure and not being able to achieve the happiness that society has determined as succes, is constantly on the increase. Many blame their past, what they didn't get as children and the lack of opportunities afforded them throughout their lifetimes. Just as many others have become angry with God and hate themselves for not having reached goals they felt were not for them or impossible to reach.

Man has not undertood that the spiritual world is more real than the natural world that we see with our own eyes. This is used by the enemy f our souls whose only objective is to destroy human beings so that they will never reach the original purpose for which they were created by God. It is time we examine ourselves and see what we are hiding in the caves of our hearts so that we may be completely free. It is time to come honest before God and acknowledge that there are areas of our lives that have not been treated by the Divine Healer. It is time to lift our eyes to Heaven and ask God to come and restore what has been destroyed in our lives and families for many years because of resentments.

This book will help you to be free froom resentment and to understand why it has manifested throughout your life and previous generations. It is time to be loosed from this evil that afflicts our society, and that you may experience true freedom. This can only can only be attained when we recognize that we need to get out of the place where we have been stuck.

In Christ,
Apostle, Dr. Sergio Enriquez
Ebenezer Ministries

INTRODUCTION

Our present day culture suffers from the ill effects of negative waves produced in previous decades. Today, hatred and vengeance are not just exclusively rooted in marginal segments of society such as organized crime, but are striking even our families and entire nations. The family unit, like a tiny cell within planet Earth, is severely affected by widespread emotional instability within its members, marital breakups and mental imbalances. Driven to extremes, these dysfunctions produce a depression so deep that in many cases they can lead to suicide.

Through His Word, God reveals to us the process by which these traits, birthed from emotioal wounds, are transformed from resentment into hate. We have no doubts that in many instances the process begins with a simple misunderstanding or unfinished interactions that function like unsigned documents. As years pass, the negativity accumulates and eventually reaches down like a root deep into the heart of man. Anchoring in unforgiveness, like the breakup in relationship between two brothers, the byproduct of resentment can lead to actual physical separation between individulas and an ensuing hidden hatred.

Throughout the pages of this book we will explore the painful process of resentment and how it reaches down from generation to generation. In the nefarious end, resentment transforms into a terrible obsession as mentioned by the Apostle John in 1 John 3:15, "whoever hates his brother is a murderer."

In our present age, the memories of past ethnic and racial contentions seem to form an ever widening, dividing gap. As we analize the development of these wounds, it is important that we keep in mind that ofenses develop into anger, to that add unforgiveness, which results in bitterness, then more anger, more resentment, more distancing and at the very end we have the sum, which is full fledged hatred.

In the Bible, we find the beginning and the end of this spirit of hatred, and we learn how it grew across the many generations until it became a great dragon. Love, on the other hand, is the language of God, and it is in that love that we must be perfected. If the true love of God which casts out all fear is not present deep within the caverns of the heart, frustration and resentment will make their way inside in a subtle and undetected manner, until they develop into hatred. We are living in very decisive times, in which we will need to make the decisions that can bring about genuine change, and that is to become a new creation.

Forgiveness is much more than a high standard of good conduct. It is more than an expression of courtesy and good manners. It is the way to bless those who curse us and to do good to those who hurt us.

As you read this book, you will understand how to get rid of and be free of resentments. These negative emotions inside the souls of men are so harmful, that they are capable of contiminating families, church congregations, whole groups of people and even entire nations.

1

GENERATIONAL
HATRED

*...discover the hatred hidden
inside the heart*

Everything began in the beginning of the year 2009, when we felt persecution and oppression knocking at the door of our church and our lives. What began as sporadic attacks of slander and character assassination in our ministry in Broward, Florida, grew in the month of July of that same year, to unprecedented levels. Flyers, letters, e-mails, even CDs strategically placed on the vehicles belonging to members of our church, all denoted hatred towards us. As an ministers of the Gospel in an apostolic and prophetic ministry, the aggression was personal.

This nefarious opposition continued as the e-mail poured in to our leaders and members of the congregation. More and more insidious messages were arriving daily, filled with lies about the ministry and work that we have been doing for more than forty years of pastoring and ministering.

The onslaught would not let up. The e-mails came from different sources, but were headed by one individual. The goal was to attack us constantly to the point of debilitating those who were younger in the faith. They would launch direct assault against the biblical teachings that we were preaching, inciting doubts on basic Bible doctrines

Many Christians started to feel weakened in their faith and doubts crept up. Others did not know how to endure. Between the months of May and August, the increase of these e-mails became like missiles into people's minds. This frontal attack and its venom were unstoppable, and since their objective was to throw a veil of mistrust over the testimony of the pastors and leaders, many believed the lies and stopped congregating.

As a reaction to the severe emotional pressures, we decided to double up on our prayers and to proclaim a fast for the Lord to reveal to us the source behind all of this. In one specific time of intercession, the Lord showed me that we were to read out loud the different biblical texts that referred to God's judgment against EDOM. We read verse by verse, and in more than one reading, we saw God's reproach to the spirit of hatred and vengeance.

During the time that we had been pastoring in Broward, Florida, there were many principalities that we discovered and had to deal with as a church. Yet, we had never directly faced the spirit of hatred. The proclaimed Word is very powerful, as it is real in the spiritual world and the demons believe and tremble before it.

While praying in the spirit I was able to understand that resentment hides in the cave of EDOM and, for that permanent and hidden hatred towards his brother God could not accept him. I saw the justice of God and how He could always see much further than what men could see. He had to reject Esau because he hated his own brother Jacob. As I saw a great truth, I perceived divine justice. I suddenly understood why there are families that have remained divided for years. It was due to this spirit of hatred which hides in the caves of people's hearts. The mount of EDOM is the opposite of the mount of God (Zion). Many Christians are religiously seated in the mount of resentment.

From that moment on, I began to deepen my study of the subject. During one particular time of worship, I heard in the spirit the word "agaita." I began to investigate in dictionaries and other sources of information, until I discovered that Agag was a distant branch from the seed of hate and persecution towards the people of God. During the beginning of he month of August, in the spirit I had a vision of a black horse go by. Its form was like a fluttering flag. It came out suddenly and sped across, looking like a trail of black, undulating smoke. Another intercessor had the same vision.

I prayed for the Lord to reveal and show me the significance of what I had seen. I was only sure of one thing; that it was a principality that had come from the spiritual world.

At that time, there was a great fear taking hold of the population regarding the H1N1 virus, but I knew that this was stronger than a plague. I understood in my spirit that this principality was fast as the wind and at the same time black as death. I was also convinced that it was not the black horse mentioned in Revelations that will gallop over mankind.

I could feel that it was temporary and that it came to attack the church. This horse rushed out all of a sudden like a wind and was coming to quench the faith of the heirs of salvation. The spirit of slander was joined with hatred and vengeance and it was gaining strength.

Around this very same time, we had returned from a missionary trip to Catania, Sicily, Italy, birthplace of the mafia. In my heart, while I had been walking through the dark, old streets of the city, I thought about the hatred and slaughter that had taken place there. This gave me the inspiration to dig deeply into the power of ambition and to what degree hatred and death were related to one another. Interestingly, the shield of Sicily is a woman's head with snakes and three legs. The feet are all going in the same direction as if it were a moving wheel. While there we would stay up all night in order to pray more than three straight hours, and I could see how that head with snakes ran all over the world.

Spiritually, hatred, vengeance and death, unite in ht spiritual world and act like a real "Mafia." We could feel in our spirit that changes in the spiritual realms had already begun, but now we had to know what kind of changes we were facing and how we should act before them. One thing I was certain, and that was that these changes were being permitted by God and men had absolutely nothing to do wit it.

In the year 2008, prophet Cindy Trimm had prophesied the following:

> "We have entered a new season. It is a season highlighted with changes. The changes are an easy dynamic. Many people pray for changes, but when they come, in some way they find spiritual resistance.
>
> Change needs an agent, what causes it, an intermediary for that change. To change, we need to actively participate in the process. Sometimes God has to light prophetic fires or allow storms to come to our lives so that we can consciously choose to cooperate with Heaven's agenda.
>
> God spoke a word to me about the Body of Christ. He told me that in this season of transition and change, there would be about forty changes.

During this time, He will cause:

1. The mantles of the sons of the sons of Issachar, Elijah and (Hannah), will be loosed over the Body of Christ. (Anointing and revelation to understand the times).

2. New wine, which symbolizes the fresh revelation from the Holy Spirit and His revival.

3. New oil, a symbol of the new anointing that will be manifested.

The implication is that we need to cooperate responsibly with the will, plans and purposes of God until we change the manner in which we live and do the work of ministry.

We have reached a new cycle and station. We shall be synchronized with the sequence and seasons of "divine times." In addition, we have seen the Serpentine spirit that has prevailed over many cities. This spirit swallows blessings, paralyzes and cauterizes growth within leadership, poisoning the minds of all the members, causing a financial, spiritual and numerical diminishing and opening up doors for the spirits of Jezebel, Ahitophel, Absalom, Haman, Sanballat and Tobiah to govern.

This is a time of intense prophetic intercession. We will see miraculous breakthroughs and manifestations if we continue to put pressure in the heavens by means of prayer.

When the enemy shall come in like a flood, the Spirit of the Lord shall lift up a standard against him. Isaiah 59:19

I have come to your side to strengthen and thicken the hedge around you. In this season, God is looking for those who would cooperate with heaven through prayer. These prayers will cause a hastening. In this year it is time to bring manifestation to life, liberty, fruition, and the activation of the atomic power of prayer."

Believing this word, we began to discern that God was going to be shaking nations, but that He would also be examining His scales to weigh the hearts. This clear vision of the divine balance was given to Tatiana Figueroa, our ministry intercessor and who along with her husband is a leader of JVH Network. She describes what God showed her as follows:

"I saw an enormous golden balance and next to it two angels. The one on the right side had a notebook where he was making notations, and the one on the left was taking people's hearts and weighing them. I saw a long line of people below the altar, and the angel was taking their hearts and placing them in the balance...it was a very large balance, perfect and solid gold.

That angel would tell the other one the precise weight of each heart, but it was given in percentages, consisting of love, repentance and devotion. The angel would write down in his notebook. I got up close and noticed that everything was written meticulously...and I heard the voice of God say:

'I am now demanding and weighing your hearts...I am a just God...I will bring a cloak of love and unity so that revival will flow in perfect synchronization...anointing for the Body, of unity, of love, of teamwork...'

We have to have a reverential fear of God...we are weighed and measured by what we speak...by what we pray, by our love, and above all, by our repentance. God weighs us all the same because he is no respecter of persons...the Lord is weighing our spirits..."

"All the ways of a man are clean in his own sight, But the Lord weighs the motives." Proverbs 16:2

THE HOLY SPIRIT GAVE ME CONFIRMATION THAT HE WOULD PROVE EVERY HUMAN BEING AND WEIGH THE INTENTIONS OF THE HEARTS.

Right along with everything that was happening in our midst, the state of Florida was facing strong economic hardships. The unemployment index had reached 11%. To this situation, we had to add not only the spiritual battle in which we were engaged, but the wave of persecution that rose against immigrants of Hispanic origin.

As pastors, the Word of God kept coming to mind to strengthen us as pastors: *"I also will keep you from the hour of testing, that hour which is about to come upon the whole world, to test those who dwell on the earth." Revelations 3:10*

During that strong period of intercession in the month of August of that ear, I was able to see how a great volcano was raising out of the earth; its crater was a mouth out of which it spoke to me. As I was looking at it, that spirit was saying to me: "I hate all of you,... I hate all of you." Thus, I would pray in the spirit so that the Lord would help me and give me the right words to rebuke it.

I only remembered that the spirit of rebellion and hatred towards authorities was seen through Korah, a prince and head of a large family throughout Moses' leadership. His attitude before God, more than before his leader, was punished by the Lord, since earth itself opened up and swallowed him alive. I told him in the spirit: "Earth is going to open up and swallow you, you cannot go against God's authority..."

The spiritual dragon is the principality that attacks the minds of people from the air. Human beings are being oppressed in their thoughts precisely by ideologies and thought waves. The minds of children, young people and adults are being assaulted twenty-four hours a day. Even at night time, wicked dreams are sent to attack as nightmares.

The spirit of disobedience is operating from the air, moving like a whirlwind, it connects with the spirits of the earth and the seas. The spirit of human ideologies, is the spirit of lies that invades the little faith of people and chokes it amidst all the social pressures. It operates in the mind by confusing childhood faith.

These ideologies also divide human groups, and have been the cause of many great wars and slaughter all through history.

What is an Ideology?

An ideology is a group of social, economic or political philosophies, ideas and values, that shape and form the basis for the way that a person or group thinks. The preservation of social or political ideas, are conservative ideologies. A transformation from established ideologies can be any of the following: radical, sudden, revolutionary, gradual and pacific.

Ideologies are usually composed of two elements: a representation of a system and a program of action. The first provides a particular point of view of reality, seen from a certain perspective. These are preconceived notions or intellectual mindsets held over established systems, which are usually compared to some alternative system, whether real or imagined. The second component has as its goal to bring the real and existing systems, as close as possible to what is perceived as the ideal system.

Ideologies characterize various groups, whether these be social groups, institutions, or a political, religious or cultural movement. Starting with Eden, the serpent was able to deceive Eve by means of a thought pattern that was contrary to God's.

Today, people's minds are saturated with fantasy. From the time we learn to read, we begin to receive a tremendous amount of information, much of which stems from the imagination of the authors, as in the case of children's books.

For instance, the first thing a small child hears are fairy tales, fables, talking animals, magical worlds, all sorts of things that do not exist anywhere except in the imagination of the authors. At school, children also learn through books that open up their minds to fantasy.

These ideologies damage true faith, choking the Word of God, which sometimes never c0omes. Unconsciously, in the mind begins the battle against the knowledge of the truth.

I ask you a question: Where do the currents of thought come from? These began in the imaginations of men, some from intellectual reasoning, but the majority of times they come from "false enlightenment." Those who say they have been "enlightened," assure that just as fallen angels in antiquity and as sons of God, anyone can receive extra sensory messages by means of meditation or yoga. Behind these ideologies there have been great discrepancies and even wars.

LET US NOT FORGET THAT SATAN CAME TO STEAL, KILL AND DESTROY. HE KNOWS THAT THE REWARDS FOR DISOBEDIENCE IS SPIRITUAL DEATH, AND IF POSSIBLE, PHYSICAL AS WELL.

How many people are living in spiritual death and don't know it? Every person who is disobedient to the laws of God and who has not been redeemed by the Blood of Jesus, is living in a state of spiritual death.

Originally, this occurred when Adam believe the "idea" brought by the fallen angel. Ideologies have always tried to annul the truth and have brought spiritual death. For centuries, this has been the number one enemy of faith.

How Can an Ideology Affect Our Society at Large?

Karl H. Marx (1818 - 1883) was a philosopher, historian, sociologist, economist, writer and thinker, German and of Jewish origin. He was at the same time, the father of scientific socialism and of communism. His ideologies caused revolutionary changes that lead to the creation of communism. This caused millions of deaths and widespread atheism. Marx is just an example of how a simple ideology can be an influence in gubernatorial systems and at the same time cause the deaths of millions of innocent people.

It is these kinds of ideologies that are behind untold number of genocides in different cultures and countries. These are the wars, like the First and Second World Wars, and civil wars as in the case of Colombia, Nicaragua and various African countries. These wars have divided countries politically and ravaged entire families. Marxist ideologies and communism form just one part of world violence. Other ideologies, like extreme Islam, also help widespread hatred towards "infidels", (although they claim their sacred book, the Koran, teaches the opposite).

We know that this is accomplished through international terrorism, that uses this religious ideology in order to forcibly impose their thinking on people by means of terror. Thus we can conclude, that although these human ideologies are different in nature, they are never the less unified by one denominator: hatred.

Why Does Man Hate Man?

This question concerning hatred in mankind is leading academia to take this problem very seriously. Why did the Nazis hate the Jews? Or why do the Hutu hate the Tutsi in Central Africa? These and other questions have never before been truly investigated. Currently, Jim Mohr, of Gonzaga University in Spokane, Washington, director of the *Institute for Action Against Hate*, has developed a new career program focused on this subject. Their objective is to find the answers to this condition which has beset mankind since ancestral times. "What generates this feeling of hate?", asks Mohr, "…and how can we overcome it?"

Gonzaga University founded this institute a decade ago, after some African-American students received some threatening letters. They also began to publish a newsletter on the subjects of intolerance and hate; *The Journal of Hate Studies*. They also organized a conference dealing with his subject matter, and offered it as a course of studies for the first time. "Our hope is that other universities will begin to imitate them", said Ken Stern, of the American Jewish Committee in New York, who has participated in this initiative. "We want to approach this subject of hatred from a more intelligent perspective," he said.

Stern, who has spent twenty years combating anti-Semitism, said the need to study this subject became much more pressing with the appearance of new organizations like *Aryan Nations*, which started to flourish in the region some years ago. Almost immediately, a resistance movement sprang up, that he hardly knew how to overcome, said Stern. The expert says there is hardly an adequate definition for the nature of hatred.

None the less, we can try to define hatred in the following manner:

Hatred is the result of accumulated resentments in the life of an individual. Negative emotions that have accumulated and serve to generate intense dislikes, desires for vengeance, unforgiveness or repulsion towards a person or situation. It is defined as an emotion contrary to love.

Love, desires the well being and the very best for the object of that love. Hate, only thinks unrest and damage. The person who has hate always projects a hostile, aggressive and repulsive conduct to the object of his hatred.

When people are bound by hatred, it is hard for them to forget perpetrations against them, therefore love and forgiveness have no place in them. Scientific studies have demonstrated that persons who hold grudges inside, get to where they can begin to suffer illnesses and mental diseases. A very important part in the healing process of these diseases, depends a great deal on starting a process that allows them to leave the past behind.

Some years ago, when I was ministering at a revival in the city of Torrejon de Ardoz, near Madrid, Spain, a woman began to manifest signs of demonic possession and I could see how this spirit was resisting leaving her. I asked the Holy Spirit to show me what was happening, and the Lord showed me clearly that she had deeply hated another person for many years. When we spoke with her, she told us that even if she were to go to hell, she would continue to hate that person and would never forgive. She preferred to make a death covenant with Satan than to forgive the person who had hurt her.

Bondages in a person's life makes them not want to get rid of negative feelings that sear them and stand in the way of their being free in the spirit. We can then see people who are bitter, frustrated, full of rancor and unhappiness because they have refused to forgive and heal those open wounds of the past. The consequences of not wanting to be free are worrisome in any life.

On the other hand, I remember an occasion in which we were ministering in a healing and miracle revival in Asturias, Spain, when someone brought an elderly woman up. She was blind and in a wheel chair. When I began to pray, I could see a very different attitude in her towards being restored of her emotions, and consequently being healed in her body. At the appropriate time, I got close to pray and the Holy Spirit said to me: "Do not pray for her, but tell her to renounce the spirit of hate that has made her sick and bound." When I told this woman what had been revealed to me, she began to cry and answered me: "It's true, I have hated my sister for more than thirty years, and since then I have been getting sicker by the day, until I've gotten into this condition this condition I'm in now." Then I was able to say to her: "The time is now for you to forgive her and renounce the spirit of hatred that you have carried for so many years." When she did so, I rebuked what had bound her and the woman jumped out of the wheel chair; her eyes were opened up and she was able to see clearly. She began to run all over the field where we were.

It is of immense importance to activate forgiveness in human beings. Millions would be set free completely of so many chains of oppression that have kept them in bondage for a lifetime.

Anger and Hatred Walk Together

Hate is a consequence of anger. When resentment is reasoned with and is allowed into wrong thinking, hatred rises up. We then have people who have everything that surrounds them and who feel bitter towards everything and towards themselves, to the point of wanting death.

The Bible teaches with how to deal with hatred, in a way that does not imprison the feelings, values or self-esteem of anyone. The only way to be free is when the key of forgiveness and love is activated.

Forgiveness is more than a lofty manner of showing good behavior. It is much more than an expression of courtesy and good manners. It is to bless those who curse us and to do good to those that despitefully hurt us.

2

XENOPHOBIA

...hatred of foreigners

In Spain, a referee interrupts a soccer game. Why? Because many spectators are insulting a player from Cameron who was threatening to abandon the field.

In Russia, aggressions against Africans, Asians and Latin Americans have become a daily occurrence. In that country there were 3,940 registered racial attacks, a 55% increase over the previous year.

In Great Britain, a third of Asians and Africans who participated in a poll confirmed that maintained they had been let go of their employment because of racial discrimination. These examples only highlight a global tendency.

When we read in the newspapers that the cases of racial discrimination and xenophobia are on the increase the world over, it begs the question: "Why have these cases multiplied to such an alarming rate and why is there so much indifference regarding it?"

Navi Pillay, United Nations Commissioner for Human Rights, stated during a press conference that took place on December 10th of 2009, that it is impossible to demolish discrimination by closing your eyes and hoping it will go away, since "indifference is discrimination's best friend." She was completely right.

Xenophobia, (from the Greek ξένος [xeno] = foreigner, and φοβία [phobia] = fear) means hatred and fear of strangers and foreigners. Manifestations range from rejection, manifested to varying degrees, to contempt and threats, all the way to violence, physical attacks and murder. One of the most common forms of xenophobia takes the form of racism. Europe is one of the places where anti racial activities have had a notable increase in recent years. It is no secret that one of the countries with greatest incidents of xenophobia in the world is Spain. The hatred towards foreigners living in that country has the international community concerned, yet remains undaunted by the photographic images which go around the world, of young people abusing immigrants in schools, trains or soccer games.

Not too long ago, a thirty-two year old Colombian was sprayed with gasoline and set on fire in a train station in the town of Arganda del Rey, near Madrid, simply because he was a South American. The deeply rooted generational hatred and racial intolerance makes these people unable to reason the motives for their actions. Their exclusionary resentments towards others are based on resentments they cannot even understand themselves.

Xenophobia has spread its seeds of hate all over the world, crimes against a part of the population that feel fearful and vulnerable for their differences are on the rise. It is common four these groups of people to be oppressed because they think different, look different, have a different skin color or religion, gender or disability.

The high index of migratory populations that go from country to country in search of a better lifestyle, has provoked the increase in hate crimes. The countries that are intolerant of the influx of other communities into their lands, feel a threat to their own ethnic roots and personal security. The downturn of global economy has exacerbated these fears. The abuse towards illegal laborers and their low wages, (especially towards women) have reached a level of exploitation, even though it is illegal to do so. The problem is no one complains. Who will take them into consideration if they don't mater?

It is common to find that cases of xenophobia or intolerance are not reported to competent authorities when they happen, because the victims do not find the opportune assistance when they turn to the criminal justice system. There are no clear laws and there is no legal definition of hate crimes within international law. In fact, the words "xenophobia" and "racial intolerance" are terms whose definitions do not even appear.

People attacked by xenophobic hatred should approach the primary means of protection, namely the local police, but they do not ordinarily do it. Generally, the victims do not inform the police for shame or fear of them, or because they do not think that what they say will be taken seriously. The police don't know what to do because there actually aren't any clear laws. However, victims of these types of crimes usually need medical assistance, psychological and spiritual support, in addition to legal council.

Racial hatred, xenophobia and every form of intolerance constitute a very grave problem of global proportions. It will be a serious threat to the world if the international community does not take steps to abolish it. The level and intensity of violence in some areas force many to leave their country of origin in order to find refuge and exile in other countries.

The Media and Xenophobia

The new forms of intolerance have found their greatest means of expression through electronic media outlets. Racist and hateful messages on the Internet have subtly infiltrated in social networks such as Facebook, which is followed by more than four hundred million people world wide. Here, hate perpetrators find others with whom to spread their hatred at the speed of light.

With just a click of the mouse and touch on a keyboard, phrases loaded with violence, death and destruction towards anyone who looks or thinks differently, are disseminated everywhere. It is a monster that can never be satisfied. Hatred has no frontiers, no boundaries, and it uses the advanced platforms of mass communication to provoke its murderous ill will, vengeance, violence and immorality towards a population that feels powerless and unprotected in their human rights.

Hatred towards women, which are before society the reflection of defenselessness and vulnerability, hatred towards Christians, the hatred of the Western world or the Jews, is a plan devised by the kingdom of darkness to widen an already separate and divided society.

It is not necessary to watch the news on television in order to be aware of the chilling truth of what is entering into homes and forming part of the subconscious. Enmeshed within scenes of violence, assassinations, persecutions, immoral radio and television commercials, are things that encourage hatred and persecution of the weakest among us. They slowly chip away at the collective consciousness in a society that does not have the time to process these messages, and believes everything they are told.

A personality of a very famous radio program in the

United States, began to make disparaging and mocking remarks over Mexican illegal workers in the country. He would say that they needed to be chased down, rounded up and kicked out of the country any way possible. It took no time for public outrage over these comments on the airwaves. However, he responded by saying that he was free to say whatever he wanted, and it was just a joke. He never apologized for his antagonistic words towards a community that is so severely attacked, as are the Hispanics living in the US, and where hate crimes towards them has multiplied.

In the year 2008, the FBI reported twenty four incidents of hate crimes, however, the Bureau for Justice Statistics reported a number seven times higher. That is to say, an average of one hundred and fifty incidents daily, where the majority of these cases are of ethnic aggression towards Hispanics. All incidents of xenophobia and racial hatred should be investigated as soon as they are reported, in order to immediately counteract any false and harmful information against the attackers. Not correcting false information on time can negatively affect public opinion and validate the false report.

Racism and Xenophobia

Racism can be closely related to, and be confused with, xenophobia, which as we have already stated, is the hate, repulsion and hostility towards foreigners. However, there are certain differences between these two concepts, since racism is an ideology of superiority, while xenophobia is an attitude of rejection. In addition, xenophobia is directed only towards foreigners, as opposed to racism. Racism is also related to other concepts with which they are sometimes confused, such as ethnocentrism, caste systems, class hierarchy, colonialism and even male superiority...

What is the root of this phenomenon? What does the Bible say about it? How can we avoid intolerant attitudes? Is it realistic to expect that mankind will leave in peace someday? The Bible offers interesting responses to these questions posed by human beings.

In *Genesis 8:21*, the Bible declares: *"the intent of man's heart is evil from his youth."* There are many individuals that enjoy oppressing others, thus confirming what is so clearly stated in *Ecclesiastes 4:1*, when it says: *"And behold I saw the tears of the*

*oppressed and that they had no one to comfort them;
and on the side of their oppressors was power, but they
had no one to comfort them."*

The Bible tells us very clearly and in no uncertain
terms, that ethnic hatred is not a recent
development, but has its roots before the birth of
Christ. In chapter one of the book of Exodus, we
see how a Hebrew named Jacob enters Egypt with
his whole family and at that point the Pharaoh
accepts them. However, time goes by and that
family grows in great numbers. More years pass
and another Pharaoh comes into power who felt
threatened when he saw the large number of
Hebrew men. This is when he decides to order
overseers of forced laborers with the intent of
oppressing the Hebrews. He did not want the
population to continue growing, so he reaches the
extreme of proclaiming death to any male child
born to the descendants of Jacob.

On the other hand, the Bible explains that there is a
much deeper reason for the problem and explains
why some ethnicities oppress others. We read in *1
John 4:8*: *"The one who does not love does not know
God, for God is love."* If anyone says, "I love God,"
and yet, he is hating his brother, he is a liar. *"For*

49

anyone who does not love his brother, whom he has seen, cannot love God, whom he has not seen." 1 John 4:20

This declaration identifies the root of ethnic intolerance: People are intolerant because they have not gotten to know or love God, whether they claim to be religious or not.

How can ethnic harmony and the fact that people should genuinely know and love God be promoted? Can the Word of God bring such conviction to them that they would desist hurting those that to them seem different?

The only book capable of revealing that knowledge is the Bible, for it teaches that God is the Father of all of mankind. *"yet for us there is but one God, the Father, from whom are all things and we exist for Him."* 1 Corinthians 8:6 Besides, it also indicates that He: *"From one man he made every nation of men, that they should inhabit the whole earth;"* Acts 17:26

Although all ethnic groups may feel proud over God giving them life, there is something about their past that they should feel regret. The apostle

Paul points it out this way: *"sin entered the world through one man"* Romans 5:12 Thus, *"for all have sinned and fall short of the glory of God."* Romans 3:23

It is wonderful to understand that God is the creator of diversity, for there are no two human beings that are exactly alike. Notwithstanding, He has never given any ethnic group reasons to feel superior over any other. The generalized idea that one ethnic group is better than others contradicts the facts that are presented in the Holy Scriptures.

There are those who ask if God Himself didn't establish ethnic prejudice when He favored Israelites and told them to keep separate from other nations (see *Exodus 34:12*).

It is true that in antiquity God chose Israel as His special group. But why? Because of Abraham's faith, the ancestor of the Israelites. God Himself governed and designated their leaders, handing them a series of laws to follow. As long as they were following the divine guidance, other groups were able to witness the result of God's government as opposed to man's.

God also showed Israel that they needed a sacrifice so that mankind could recover their good relationship with Him. Therefore, what He did with that nation, benefited all nations. This lines up with what was promised to Abraham in *Genesis 22:18: "In your seed all the nations of the earth shall be blessed, because you have obeyed My voice."*

Likewise, the Jews had the privilege of receiving God's declarations and to become the people out of whose bosom the Messiah was born. This honor was given to them in order that all nations on earth would benefit. This fulfilled what the Sacred Scriptures had foretold, that there would be a time when all people, all ethnic groups, would receive great blessings.

Many nations will come and say, "Come, let us go up to the mountain of the Lord, to the house of the God of Jacob.

He will teach us his ways, so that we may walk in his paths."

The law will go out from Zion, the word of the Lord from Jerusalem.

He will judge between many peoples and will settle

disputes for strong nations far and wide. They will beat their swords into plowshares and their spears into pruning hooks.

Nation will not take up sword against nation, nor will they train for war anymore.

Every man will sit under his own vine and under his own fig tree, and no one will make them afraid, or the Lord Almighty has spoken. Micah 4:2-4

Although Jesus Christ preached to the Jews, He also foretold: *"This gospel of the kingdom shall be preached in the whole world as a testimony to all the nations, and then the end will come." Mathew 24:14*

In conclusion, no people would be excluded. As you can see, God gives us a perfect example on how to deal with all ethnic groups without playing favorites. He is impartial, as a result everyone who reveres Him and is righteous before Him is accepted (see *Acts 10:34-35*).

In the same manner, the laws that God gave ancient Israel shows us that He cares about every group and nation. Now, observe how the Law required more than to simply tolerate foreigners living in the country:

'The stranger who resides with you shall be to you as the native among you, and you shall love him as yourself, for you were aliens in the land of Egypt; I am the Lord your God." Leviticus 19:34

Many of the laws that God established taught the Israelites to be kind to immigrants. This is why when Boaz saw a needy foreign woman gleaning in his field, he followed the divine instructions and made sure his reapers left enough sprigs for her to gather (see *Ruth 2:1, 10, 16*).

Jesus taught like no one lese about man's relationship to God. He directed His disciples to be kind to whomever was different. He spoke with a Samaritan woman and she was surprised herself that He would talk to her, for the Samaritans were an ethnic group that were despised by the Jews. During the conversation, Jesus helped her kindly to understand how to reach eternal life, and how to be free of the ethnic hatred that was oppressing her (*see John 4:7-14*).

In a clear and objective manner, Jesus also illustrated the manner in which to treat persons of other ethnicities through the parable of the good Samaritan. This man had found a Jew seriously wounded by some assailants. Upon seeing him, he probably reasoned: "Why should I help a Jew when they despise my people?" And yet, the individual mentioned here had a very different opinion to the others who had passed by and seen the man. Contrary to other travelers who had walked past the victim without stopping to help, the Samaritan shuddered and was moved to compassion, helping in every way he could. Jesus concluded His parable by saying that whoever wanted the favor of God would have to do the same (see *Luke 10:30-37*).

The apostle Paul taught that anyone seeking to please God had to change their character and thought patterns and imitate God with regards to others.

"Do not lie to one another, since you laid aside the old self with its evil practices, and have put on the new self who is being renewed to a true knowledge according to the image of the One who created him-- a renewal in which there is no distinction between Greek and Jew, circumcised and uncircumcised, barbarian, Scythian, slave and freeman, but Christ is all, and in all.

So, as those who have been chosen of God, holy and beloved, put on a heart of compassion, kindness, humility, gentleness and patience; bearing with one another, and forgiving each other, whoever has a complaint against anyone; just as the Lord forgave you, so also should you. Beyond all these things put on love, which is the perfect bond of unity." (*Colossians 3:9-14*)

Anyone having true knowledge of God and His Word will change completely. Is it true that anyone who gets to have a relationship with God changes the way they treat persons of other ethnic groups?

It is a stunning fact that ought not be overlooked, that today in fulfillment of the Bible prophecy, true worship is bringing together millions of people from all nations, tribes, peoples and tongues (see *Revelations 7:9*).

They are all waiting to see how love will replace hatred in a global society, a society in which we will soon see the fulfillment of what God promised Abraham: All of the families on earth will be blessed (see *Acts 3:25*).

God has never given any ethnic group reason to feel superior to others. By the term 'ethnic group', we are referring to a community of individuals who stand out from others by having common bonds of race, nationality, religion, language or culture. Wherever the grace and love of God is not present, there is bitterness and resentment which lead to manifestations of hatred and vengeance. On the other hand, when the love of God is affirmed and embraced, forgiveness flourishes like an inextinguishable source of answers for all who so desire it.

3

OUR CULTURE'S DESTRUCTIVE PATH

...from anger to hate

*H*e who hates disguises it with his lips, but he lays up deceit in his heart. When he speaks graciously, do not believe him, for there are seven abominations in his heart. Though his hatred covers itself with guile, His wickedness will be revealed before the assembly. Proverbs 26:24-26 (NASB)

We are living in a society, which has lost its basic moral principles and has discarded true morality, found only in the character of God our Creator. The world has turned its back on God and told Him "we want to have nothing to do with you." To use as an example, let us look back and examine recent past events in the United States alone, so that we can get a sense of what has been taking place in our world.

Statistics for the Beginning of 2009

Many different acts of violence are included in the category of hate crimes and are punishable by law, (as long as judge and/or jury are not racists and rule justly). In the beginning of 2009, there was a hate crime committed every hour in the United States. We may ask ourselves, what is a hate crime?

A hate crime is defined as any violent act committed against another because of his race, color, place of origin, nationality, sexual orientation, sex, political affiliation, etc.

- In the majority of cases, hate crimes are not reported properly because the victims choose to remain silent.
- The law can protect citizens effectively, as long as victims report the crimes and are willing to participate in the due legal process and testify against the perpetrators.
- Hate crimes violate the victim's civil rights.
- Victims of hate crimes often suffer from fear, humiliation and feel defenseless.

Incidents Motivated by Prejudice:

- Written or spoken threats or constant intimidation.
- Vandalism or destruction of property.
- Physical assault or death threats.

Not all incidents driven by hate are crimes. Verbal insults, although offensive, are not considered a crime unless it is accompanied by a violent threat and the ability to carry it out.

In the beginning of the year, hatred increased in the United States to unimaginable heights. The world over was hoping for "change" after the start of an economic recession in the country, and the target for that hope was placed in the new American president. Later, this same event opened up the hidden wounds of racism along with the memories of slavery in the 17th and 18th century, which was as prevalent in the United States as in other colonies from Spain, England, Italy and other countries. We cannot ignore the cultural and racial problems that these countries have had to endure. Hatred has always been the result of extreme actions perpetrated against a given group by another.

In order to understand the roots of hatred we need to go back to its beginnings, the cause. Anger is the tool that opens the door to hatred. If we pay attention, we will see how even a small incident causing resentment can develop into a feeling of vengeance, all because of suppressed anger. Suspicions, contempt, anger and wrath all separate and cause divisions. At the individual level, the physical and emotional separation of those who were at one time friends, family or spouses, produces a sense of loss in the human being that is akin to spiritual death.

On many occasions, human beings who have suffered a rift in their relationships stay together out of necessity, but in the meantime the friendship and trust have died, the love is over, conversations come to a dead stop. Unfortunately, no one is exempt from having to suffer some of these situations in life, but there is always room for improvement in the quality of life a person lives beyond these experiences.

In this day and age, we can see how uncontrollable hatred fills the hearts of human beings like a giant monster having no opponent to detain it. In fact, hatred has reached such proportions in recent years that it has become a pervasive evil, causing a total disregard to the rights of others and demonstrating no compassion at the suffering of fellow human beings.

Just like the human body, the human family is a body, which begins from the union of two cells to the formation of the bones, tendons, muscles and nerves that give it form. By contrast, the pulling apart of families and its relationships produces a dismemberment that is the destruction of society as a whole. When families are destroyed, man self-destructs.

Human beings are composed of a body, soul (mind-emotions-ego-will) and spirit. Where then, is the anger formed that gives rise to hate?

It begins within the spiritual heart of the person, where it remains hidden in the person's life. The spirit of anger passes from the womb into a child, clinging to the genes and taking residence in future generations.

Let us continue with recent statistics;

Hate Crimes at the End of the First Decade into the 21st Century.

Hate Crimes: Deaths not officially on an FBI list

From the AL DIA Newspaper, 11/25/09

Someone causes your death, but rejoice! It's nothing personal, no one hates you, and your death... it was not murder. At least, not officially, according to our justice system or the FBI. Setting aside natural causes or accidents, someone may take your life, but the murderer only requires a shameless judge, a passive community and a biased judge or jury. In addition, yes, perhaps you are dead, but that would be your problem, not theirs. The FBI maintains "hate crimes" statistic files since 1995. Yet the head count itself has been a less than possible task. The incidents range from rape to murder and prejudices include race, ethnicity, gender and religious denomination. The problem lies in who decides if such crimes were truly hate crimes or not. While the FBI registers an average of 24 hate crime incidents daily in its 2008 report, the Bureau of Justice Statistics reports a number some 7 times higher - by another 150 daily incidents. One of the report's authors, Michael Lieberman, spokesperson for the

Anti Defamation League in Washington said that among the more than 7,500 hate crimes documented in 2007, crimes over racial prejudices were the most common, followed by attacks connected with religion and lastly by crimes related to the victim's sexual orientation.

The study demonstrates that between 2003 and 2007 there was almost a 40% increase in hate crimes committed against Hispanics. "Of all the crimes motivated by prejudices against minorities reported in 2007, 7.8% involved Hispanics," the study pointed out. "Of all the crimes in 2007 motivated by prejudice against a victim's ethnic group or national origin, almost 60% affected Hispanics, with an almost 60% increase since 2003."

THE PRIMARY TARGET FOR HATE CRIMES IS RACIALLY MOTIVATED, SECOND ETHNIC (HISPANICS) AND THIRD, RELIGION.

The difference stems from the fact that "the FBI only counts crimes that are reported to the police... the BJS compiles information from the victims who are asked if hatred had anything to do with the crime", according to "Hate Crimes in

America", published by the National Justice Institute published in 2007. While police authorities and victims argue over whether a crime can be considered a "hate crime" or not, the United States remains a silent witness as much of its sense of security and equality for all crumbles.

Do you remember the death of Luis Ramirez, an illegal immigrant and father of two children in Shenandoah, Pennsylvania? The jury decided that the teenagers involved had not committed a "hate crime", that this could not be considered a murder, in fact, it was not even ruled aggravated assault. You be the judge if justice was served in this case after reading the following quotes from someone who took part as jury foreman. Eric Macklin on the Shenandoah case: "I believe all four boys are racist and I was pretty close to find them guilty, but due to the evidence presented I just couldn't do it. I absolutely believe it." Derrick Dunshack, - one of the perpetrators- was wearing a T-Shirt with a US Border Patrol emblem to a Halloween party, after Luis' death took place. "This goes way beyond bad taste, this is racist. That was awful!" Yes, truly awful, hatred and murder may be rampant, but remember that it is still not "official." - Taken from AL DIA

Newspaper.

Taking a Close Look at the Process

People today suffer the consequences of the absolute disregard they show one another. Hatred begins with a wound, from a senseless, emotional reaction to contempt; the wounds of rejection are the very culprits of distancing and breaking apart of relationships. Rifts between siblings are so pervasive they extend across many successive generations. In fact, these wounds to the soul are very difficult to detect but they are far more deadly than cancer. If we carefully analyze the true root of many terrible diseases, we often find underlying grudges, just one-step away from wrath. These deep-seated, turbulent emotions can cause havoc and terrible diseases in a person's body.

The soul, center of our thought and emotions, upon finding itself imprisoned, sends a message to the entire body from the brain by means of nervous impulses. It activates and transmits thoughts of worry and fear to which the body responds in recoil.

Likewise, fear is a double-edged sword, which seeks to protect but actually only unleashes blindness and confusion. This is the reason why people who become extremely angry have difficulty understanding, much less reason, when they are going through a difficult stage in their lives. When excessive emotions reach a point where they are ready to explode, the person is capable of committing any violent activity and loses all ability to make judicious decisions. Unfortunately, many divorces are decided upon at this juncture.

WITHIN DIVINE LAW, THERE IS ADVICE FOR EVERY DIFFICULT SITUATION. WE ONLY NEED TO READ IT AND PUT IT INTO PRACTICE.

God, our creator and maker of our body and soul, knows the secret of the imbalances that produce our negative emotions. This is the reason why He left us advice concerning these things so that man could avail himself of it and benefit. If heeded, man would not have to succumb to the agitated demands of unbridled feelings and emotions. One such advice reads as follows:

- *"You shall not hate your fellow countryman in your heart; you may surely reprove your neighbor, but shall not incur sin because of him."*
- *"You shall not take vengeance, nor bear any grudge against the sons of your people, but you shall love your neighbor as yourself; I am the LORD." Leviticus 19:17-18 (NASB)*

It is very important to keep all of the council of God in order to avoid painful and embarrassing situations leading us to incorrect actions. Hidden within God's advice, law and commandments are the most significant secrets to a life of health and happiness. God never recommends disdain, mockery, malicious gossip or disregard towards others. In addition, He exhorts us to act sensibly when there is a dispute amongst us. Reasoning and meditating on what has happened brings us to a place of peace and makes no room for anger or unreasonable, uncontrollable emotions.

The holding on to a grudge because of unforgiveness, will with time transform into a root of bitterness, which is very difficult to pull out. It is a serious problem of enormous proportions: a wound that has not been dealt with, deepens and widens, it grows until it shoots roots of pain, and that pain transforms into resentments and grudges. If healing does not take place at the opportune time, with the passing of years the resentment turns into hatred. These adverse emotions within the soul not only produce diseases, but since there is no genuine forgiveness residing in the heart, the person might continue to live out his life acting under complete pretenses. What follows is a life of complete inner emptiness in the heart as well as the soul.

The Consequences of Anger

When a person allows anger to develop towards another, whether it involves a relative, spouse or co-worker, it fulfills what the Apostle John says in his epistle, that the person becomes a murderer, or one who assassinates his own brother.

- *"We know that we have passed out of death into life, because we love the brethren. He who does not love abides in death."*
- *"Everyone who hates his brother is a murderer; and you know that no murderer has eternal life abiding in him." 1 John 3:14-15*

Jesus Himself referred to anger saying:

"But I say to you that everyone who is angry with his brother shall be guilty before the court." Mathew 5:22

The word "guilty," in Greek [enochos], translates as: "judged responsible or chargeable for a reprehensible act." Therefore, whatever a person's social class or condition as an individual, if he becomes angry towards his own brother, he shall be exposed and charged at God's last judgment. In this verse, Jesus was referring to the penalty that was imposed on someone who murdered another, making the comparison between a murderer and one who hates his brother; He says they are one and the same.

By using dialogue, God was teaching the religious folks of His time, the inner workings of the human heart, and the way that the sin of murder entered a person through consistent anger. Jesus was explaining that anger opens the door to hatred. In the same manner, many centuries before God tried to reason with Cain, imploring him to think and reason about what was taking a hold of his heart before taking action. He was teaching him to be careful, because if he were to "not do what is right," that is, if temptation was close by, he should be mindful of not falling into sin and "open up doors."

Lack of understanding grows inside the heart, filling it with rage. Cain completely ignored the path of dialogue and challenge to reason into which God was trying to lead him. Envy and jealousy are part of anger. This is literally what Cain manifested, and in his foolishness, he gave place to sin. With great wrath, he became the first assassin when he murdered his own brother.

Uncontrolled anger always leads to disaster. Cain's offense led him to anger, that anger ignited his wrath, changing his whole countenance. Furthermore, Cain was filled with rage and bitterness leading to deep resentment. When he distanced himself from his brother, he began to scheme his vengeance against him, until he carried out his plan for destruction.

God does not take any part in this because His very nature is love. Anger is the beginning of something totally contrary to His nature. This is why He says: "give me your heart, son." The heart is the place where plots occur that can lead a person to sin. Sin is a direct open door to spiritual death. The human heart is full of deep, dark caves unknown even to the person who carries it. Only the Lord's light, which is the only true, pure love, can shed any light into our nether regions. The heart can be compared to a dark cave, from where we discover the beginnings of hatred towards another. (Later on in the book, we will discuss the Caves of Edom)

Why Do People Become Angry with God?

Because it is easier to do so than to take full responsibility. People blame God for their financial imbalances, for their own failures and misery. When problems are on the increase, the accompanying pressures and tensions grow parallel with the inability to deal with them effectively.

BITTERNESS AND RESENTMENT ARE THE FRUIT OF ANGER; FRUSTRATION THE CONSEQUENCE.

Without realizing it, people constantly scheme in their minds and seek to find someone whom to blame for their problems. In the book of Genesis,

Be Free from Resentment

we read the story of how Adam blames his wife Eve, and in turn, she accuses the serpent.

> MAN IS ALWAYS LOOKING TO FIND SOMEONE TO BLAME FOR HIS FAILURES, BUT HE WILL NEVER ADMIT HIS OWN FAULT.

Today, history literally repeats itself. Many are blaming God for the bad things that happen to them. It is common to hear questions such as; "If God is so good, why doesn't He do something about world hunger?" Alternatively, "Why doesn't He help abandoned children?" Man in his selfishness is blind to reality. There is only one truth but disobedience renders people blind to it.

Analyzing the Heart

- *"The heart is more deceitful than all else. And is desperately sick; Who can understand it?"*
- *"I, the Lord, search the heart, I test the mind, Even to give to each man according to his ways, According to the results of his deeds."*
  Jeremiah 17:9-10

Some time ago, Stephen Hanson had a revelation

regarding the heart. This is what he says:

"I was down in the ocean waters beneath the surface looking down. Afterwards, I was in the middle of a submarine tank that was carrying people to the deep sea in order to explore it. The Lord was with me as we traveled down together. I was observing as we encountered various whirlpools and currents in the water. We were looking at the water, and yet, I knew that this was an analogy or symbol of what He was showing me about the heart. 'I have created a new heart in every man and woman. It is my abode, the place where I reside. Rivers of living water flow through it. In the sea, there are continuous currents, whirlpools and various tides. In the depths of the ocean, there are many secret places. There are places where no man has ever been. There are creatures that are unknown...but even so, I know these places because I am the one who dug out these caves and subterranean places. There are places that only I know of, I can empty these places and speak from them. I live in that secret place. These are silent places where the currents cannot invade. It is like a man who travels down to the bottom of the ocean to explore its depths. He is kept from the outer waters and is protected from the elements. That is the place where I AM.

I have explored these caves that are deep within your hearts. No one has ever reached the bottom. There are deceptions inside man that he does not know about. Yet, in spite of it all, I can still make his heart new. I can perform surgery in those areas of your heart that need work. Allow me to explore the depths of your heart with you, because it is with the heart that man believes. I can then empty it out and build an altar and a sanctuary. I will do a beautiful work in you, for I do not look at the outer appearance, but at the inner parts of the heart. Hence, you will say; the Lord has given me a brand new heart.'"

How can we be set free of this terrifying evil that has influenced human beings on this planet?

Let us begin on this long and meticulous road to discover the cave where it has hidden for centuries. Let us find it and bring it out into the light. The Holy Spirit is on hand to guide you and assist you and to help you live free in every area of your life. Sometimes it is not quite so easy to expose the intruders that have taken up space in the caves of the heart. Who are they? Moreover, how do you recognize them and drag them out into the light?

Keep reading... there is more for you in this new day.

4

THE CAVES OF EDOM

...hidden resentment inside the heart

How is it that someone can carry anger inside his or her heart for any length of time? We cannot ignore that what passes off as mere emotion and is so common between family and friends, is no less than an actual spirit of anger and resentment. The very first time that resentment is mentioned in the law of God, is in Leviticus, when God Himself teaches Moses so that he can exhort the multitude to keep His commandments.

To go against these commandments is to risk falling into disobedience, which places bondages on the soul and puts the very heart of man into prison.

You shall not take vengeance, nor bear any grudge against the sons of your people, but you shall love your neighbor as yourself; I am the LORD. Leviticus 19:18

The word "resentment" in Hebrew is [nacám], and it means: vengeance, vindictive, punishment to clear of blame. When a person allows their heart to be filled with grudges because of an unforgiven offense, even when the person is in denial, a strongman takes residence in a person's life. This spirit of anger and resentment has a secret goal of carrying out vengeance. As this spirit remains hidden, it does not come up to reasoning; therefore, the desire for vengeance is hidden under a cover of darkness. On the other hand, the opposite of resentment is love. In perfect love there is no fear; love does not seek its own, and does not bear grudges. God is love, and in Him there is no gloom or darkness. Why then, allow ourselves to live under the shadows of resentments for so long? So much pain is held onto, simply because people do not reach out to our Heavenly Father, who is the Spirit of true love.

Lack of love in a child's formative years creates a void in the young person's heart. Spirits of wickedness act by pressuring the thoughts of perverse individuals. Satan, the enemy of the human race, knows that if a child is molested or raped during his young innocent years, his personality will be gravely affected. He will enter into confusion and his personality and subconscious will become imbalanced. Such is the case of children abused by pedophiles. Without a doubt, this produces emptiness within that only the presence of God will be able to fill at the right time, whenever the person is ministered in this area. An abused child is frightened of not only being discovered, but from the intimidation perpetrated by the abuser. A person who is a prisoner of fear is bound and feels the deepest pain. From these feelings of fear, anger and resentment stem emotional imbalances that are sometimes difficult to unravel. A desire for vengeance is an intricate part of bearing a grudge, even if for practical reasons the desire is never fulfilled. These emotions will remain bound to the heart in a complex sea of instability, bringing with them burden and oppression to the soul.

Resentment's Favorite Hiding Place is the Caves of EDOM

This might well be the thought in the minds of siblings all around the world: *"So Esau bore a grudge against Jacob because of the blessing with which his father had blessed him; and Esau said to himself, "The days of mourning for my father are near; then I will kill my brother Jacob." Genesis 27:41*

The evils of enmity and resentment lie hidden in the recondite caves of the heart. Throughout history, we have witnessed families whose lives have been punctuated by hate and grudges towards each other. The never healed wounds produced by strife between siblings and relatives, in the end transform into open doors for generational spirits. In order to understand this subject better, and why we associate the caves of the heart with the caves at Edom, we shall travel to the past in the Bible. Biblically speaking, Edom is a type of the spirit of enmity, which passes from generation to generation.

Who Was Esau?

Esau, who is known as the Father of the Edomites, was the son of Isaac and Rebecca. From his mother's womb, Esau fought with his twin brother to be the first-born. The Word says the following: ..."...*But the children struggled together within her;*" *Genesis 25:22*

86

Esau had an independent spirit, which is typical for a young "rebel without a cause." His devious behavior brought "bitterness of spirit" to his parents, Isaac and Rebecca (*Genesis 26:35*). His mother suffered from his rebellious actions. Not only did he marry Hittite women (which was unlawful according to the customs of his people), but he also took Ishmael's daughter as his wife and later on went to become yoked with the daughters of the Canaanites (*Genesis 27:46, Genesis 28:9*). Esau led a tumultuous and unstable life, highlighted by the fact that he became a polygamist, something that God abhorred. Two of Israel's most bitter tribal enemies; Korah and Amalek, were birthed from among the women and concubines that he chose outside his lineage.

Esau's name was changed to Edom, which means; red. This occurred one day when he came in very tired from hunting. Jacob was cooking some lentil stew with game (red) and Esau asked for some. Jacob responded by saying that he would give him the stew if he would sell him his birthright for it, and Esau accepted. In light of these events, we ask ourselves; Could Esau have gotten angry over the exchange his brother proposed? Can something physical like eating be compared with a spiritual inheritance? Hadn't they been bickering from their mother's womb? Weren't they carrying enmity in their blood? In his heart, Esau did not esteem "God's blessing." Being the first-born placed him in line for the privilege of belonging to the genealogy of the awaited Messiah. However, Esau only gave value to those things in the present that pertained to the natural man, or the flesh. Esau was not a spiritual man.

IN A SECOND AND OUT OF NOWHERE, A GENERATIONAL RIFT CAN OCCUR BETWEEN SIBLINGS FOR SOMETHING AS SIMPLE AS A MEAL OR AN EXCHANGE OF WORDS. THE DESIRE FOR VENGEANCE COMES INTO THE HEART THROUGH UNHEALED WOUNDS, MISUNDERSTANDINGS, MOMENTS OF ANGER AND LACK OF COMMUNICATION.

The decision of the heart is expressed out of the mouth: *"The days of mourning for my father are near; then I will kill my brother Jacob."* Genesis 27:41 Enmity takes place in the heart when it gives over to resentment, which is a dangerous step away from hatred.

> **Resentment is a hidden thirst for vengeance.**

What Does Edom Represent Spiritually?

The prophet Amos predicts the punishment of Edom. Edom represents the hidden resentment within the heart towards a brother. The spirit of anger, vengeance and hatred lies hidden in the caves of Edom, having no regard for class or position. Many resentful people do not understand why God does not prosper them.

They continually complain and live lives of oppression to memories of the past. Little do they know that it is those hidden grudges they are bearing that are an impediment to receiving God's prosperity and blessings.

"Thus says the Lord, "For three transgressions of Edom and for four I will not revoke its punishment, because he pursued his brother with the sword, While he stifled his compassion; His anger also tore continually, and he maintained his fury forever." Amos 1:11

Important Lessons From the Father of Resentments

1. **He hunted his brother to kill him.** In His Word, God prohibits enmities and strife. Everyone who persists in disobedience (sins) in this area falls under a curse.
2. **He violated every principle of natural affection.**
3. **He always held rage in his heart.** This is the same attitude that constantly robs people from their blessings. The fury is inflicted by a spirit of darkness assigned to the person who will not forgive in order to oppress them and their opponents at the same time.
4. **He kept resentment in his heart perpetually.** God declares openly... vengeance is mine, I will repay. No one can take vengeance into his or her own hands, when God has said that it belongs to Him only. *Isaiah 63:1-5*

"The arrogance of your heart has deceived you, you who live in the clefts of the rock..." Obadiah 1:3

One of the sins that is hidden by "resentment" is haughtiness. This is the sin that God judges and over which Edom fell. He boasted of his own worth and mocked his brother. God could not allow his haughtiness to go higher than the throne of God. Only He is exalted (*El Eyon*). Edom joined Jacob's enemies to fight at war against his own brother. This is a tactic that God abhors, and He will not leave unpunished anyone who joins his brother's enemies in order to destroy him.

For they have conspired together with one mind; against you they make a covenant: the tents of Edom and the Ishmaelites, Moab and the Hagrites; Psalms 83:5

This psalm confirms that normally the enemy joins forces with other evil spirits in order to persecute God's people. Jacob has oftentimes been judged harshly and has been taught about as the deceiver and usurper, but we can see how from his mother's womb God calls him "he who replaces," because he would replace his brother and inherit all of the blessings chosen by God.

Why Was Edom Severly Punished by God?

The prophecy spoken by Obadiah the prophet says

as follows: *"Because of violence to your brother Jacob, you will be covered with shame, and you will be cut off forever..." Obadiah 1:10-14*

God punished Edom's sin severely. God reveals in His Word that it is important to make amends rapidly when there are disagreements and offenses amongst brethren.

Verse 12: *"**Do not gloat** over your brother's day, the day of his misfortune, and do not rejoice..."* Although Cain was not watching after his brother's moves like Esau, yet his indifference and maliciousness became a sin before God.

*"And do not **rejoice**"* anyone who delights in his heart over the downfall of his brother is in grave sin before God. The spirit that was operating on the inhabitants of Edom cheered in the day of Israel's anguish. It is in the caves of Edom that all that is dark and hidden in the heart of man makes its residence, and when that heart rejoices and delights in another person's unfortunate downfall, it becomes sin. Feeling joy and satisfaction at someone else's wretchedness is a failure that God does not tolerate.

Esau's behavior demonstrates how a spirit that delights in doing his own will (rebellion) operates. God said that His spirit would always be in direct conflict with the flesh. Edom is the spirit of hatred towards a brother, and God does not approve by virtue of the fact that He said: "You shall love your neighbor (brother, fellow man) as yourself." God is calling you to commit to Him, to obey Him unconditionally, so that you may become "God's Israel." In the case of Esau, Rebecca his mother always stood by his twin Jacob. God, in His grace, chose the second born and not the first.

The Bible clearly explains in *Romans 9:10-12: And not only this, but there was Rebecca also, when she had conceived twins by one man, our father Isaac; for though the twins were not yet born and had not done anything good or bad, so that God's purpose according to His choice would stand, not because of works but because of Him who calls, it was said to her, "THE OLDER WILL SERVE THE YOUNGER."*

Esau is the Equivalent of Our Sinful Nature.

Esau and Jacob are a type and shadow of our own condition. In Malachi 1: 1-4, there is a reference to this: *"The oracle of the word of the LORD to Israel through Malachi. 'I have loved you,' says the LORD But you say, 'How have You loved us?' 'Was not Esau Jacob's brother?' declares the LORD 'Yet I have loved Jacob; but I have hated Esau, and I have made his mountains a desolation and appointed his inheritance for the jackals of the wilderness.' Though Edom says, 'We have been beaten down, but we will return and build up the ruins'; thus says the LORD of hosts, 'They may build, but I will tear down; and men will call them the wicked territory, and the people toward whom the LORD is indignant forever."* These two characters speak to us about our own nature as individuals. Esau represents our fallen, sinful nature, while Jacob represents the opposite, the edified and restored nature according to God's model.

Remember: Esau did not take into account God's destiny or prophetic purpose for him, and he simply traded the plans that God had for him for a meal of lentils and a moment of pleasure. In the very same way, Satan tries time and time again to interfere in our lives, attempting to get us to ignore spiritual things and convince us to run from God's purposes, just as he did with Esau. He tries to get us to exchange our divine destiny for a bowl of lentils, as it were. Thus, Esau symbolizes our fallen nature, our old man, a fleshly nature, while Jacob symbolizes the new man in God. God has supernaturally placed this spiritual nature in us by grace and faith in Jesus Christ, the eternal Son. God loves the sinner, but He does not love what the sinner does which is disobedience to His law. God abhors fallen nature. Hence, the Bible declares: "...those that walk according to the flesh will never please God." As Esau represents this fallen nature manifested in fleshly sin and desires, those walking in this condition cannot please God.

Obadiah's Vision; God's Word Concerning Edom

Sometimes the spirit of resentment is closely tied to haughtiness, and the Word tells us that pride is the root of all evils. Using a tree as a metaphor, the Word shows us that the trunk is pride, Lucifer's initial sin, which in turn grows branches of anger, resentment, rejection, hatred and vengeance. It is obvious then that every human being has a battle with original sin within his or her body, and pride is at the very center of this sin. Perhaps many say... "Why, I'm not proud..." but that is because they are not aware that we are all under the curse for Adam's sin. We all struggle with this curse, which in manner of generalization we call "the flesh." On verse 4 of Obadiah 1, the prophet refers to Esau's descendants with the same expression that the prophet Ezequiel also uses to describe the spirit of haughtiness; "...*You who say in your heart...*" Therefore, we see a similarity between the way the heart is mentioned in Obadiah to the way it is mentioned in Ezequiel with regards to Edom.

Mount Zion Vs. Mountain of Esau

That confrontation which began inside of a womb will come to an end in the future, when Mount Zion, the house of Jacob, will rise to bring judgment to the house of Esau, and the Kingdom of our Lord Jesus Christ will remain forever and ever. The Lord will celebrate a day of vengeance, a year of righting all the wrongs in defense of the cause of Zion.

Isaiah 34:8 For the LORD has a day of vengeance, a year of recompense for the cause of Zion. God has established a date to bring Edom to a tribunal because He has a legal cause, a controversy with regards to Zion. The original Zion was the place for the seat of David's government, thus Zion became a symbol for the administration of the Kingdom of

God. Naturally, from the perspective of this side of the Cross, we believe that the New Jerusalem has priority over the Old Jerusalem, and in the same manner there is a "New Zion," which is different from the original location. Once we understand that the prophecies concerning Esau are subject to all these diverse names, it is evident that the Bible is full of prophecies against Esau's descendants in the last days. Many do not realize this, and yet, many prophetic declarations are directed at other names: Edom, Idumea, Seir, Teman or Amalek... *The deliverers will ascend Mount Zion to judge the mountain of Esau, and the kingdom will be the LORD'S. Obadiah 1:21*

The prophecy speaks of two mountains; God's mountain and Satan's mountain, or Mount Zion and the mountain of Esau. Mount Zion is the spiritual place where thousands of angels will congregate and which will rest over Jerusalem for a time when the King will govern the earth. The opposing mountain is Esau, a place of hatred, rejection and rebellion, inhabited by birds of prey and where there is no light, only darkness, evil and hate.

However, pelican and hedgehog will possess it, and owl

and raven will dwell in it; and He will stretch over it the line of desolation, And the plumb line of emptiness. Its nobles--there is no one there whom they may proclaim king- And all its princes will be nothing. ... The tree snake will make its nest and lay eggs there, and it will hatch and gather them under its protection. Yes, the hawks will be gathered there, every one with its kind. Isaiah 34:11-12, 15

In which mountain are you? Are you in the one of the promise, seeking an eternal inheritance, or are you in the one that only promises temporary fleshly pleasures?

THIS IS THE TIME APPOINTED FOR YOUR DECISION. DO NOT ALLOW A GRUDGE TO ROB YOU OF YOUR SPIRITUAL AND PHYSICAL INHERITANCE. FIGHT FOR YOUR INHERITANCE!

5

THE SIGNS OF TREASON

...Amalek shows up from behind

The Birth and Appearance of Amalek

Esau had a concubine (illegitimate union) who bore him a son he named Amalek. This marked the beginning of the Amalekites (See *Genesis 36:12*). The spirits of rebellion and fornication passed through the genes to his son, and this curse took force directly upon his grandson. Amalek means "cursed by God." We can glean from this that the refinement of vengeance sprang from the Esau's loins, as a result of his illegitimate relationship. While in Edom (Esau) was the dwelling for resentment, in his grandchild the curse takes on greater strength, combined with the curse of fornication, which is the opening for rebellion and anarchy. Hence, every ritual of witchcraft is initiated with an act of fornication. In the Bible narrative, we read that years after God speaks to Moses He gives him a promise for expansion into a new territory called Canaan.

In our present day, Canaan means a place of position and provision. Once you get there, you will enjoy favor and prosperity. God's objective at that point was to liberate a people from four hundred years of oppression. God was able to demonstrate to His people the wonders of His powerful hand and power by taking them to where they could cross a dry Red Sea. Yet, Pharaoh's persecution did not end there, but continued to the desert under another name, Amalek. There the Israelites found much more shrewd and astute enemies. In fact, Amalek was the first enemy that Israel had to overcome on the way to the Promised Land. They were attacked by them while they were in Rediphim, angry and murmuring against Moses.

He named the place Massah and Meribah because of the quarrel of the sons of Israel, and because they tested the LORD, saying, "Is the LORD among us, or not?" Then Amalek came and fought against Israel at Rephidim. Exodus 17:7-8

The word Meribah means, struggle (squabble,

dispute, quarrel, complaint). When a person is involved in a quarrel with another, this is when they have to be very careful, because that is the very door that the enemy will use to attack and solidify a curse. At that point, God's blessings which rain from heaven will be detained. Until the person is free from the battle, he will be exposed to a distancing from God's presence.

The Amalekites came out of nowhere and declared war on the Israelites. This is exactly what happens in real life. Many individuals do not know how to have victory over their own spiritual battles and constantly depend upon the prayers of others. And here is the key! The heart manifests rebellion through complaints and quarrels, and this makes the soul have to enter into stress and exhaustion. Amalek appears on the scene and Moses gives an order to Joshua to get ready for battle while he goes to the mount in order to intercede. This is where the battle begins. Today, in your own life, the spirit of vengeance can attack you when you are tired and grumbling spiritually.

IT WILL ALWAYS RISE AGAINST YOU JUST WHEN YOU ARE ABOUT TO ACHIEVE THE VICTORY IN THE VISION

GOD HAS GIVEN YOU. BUT WHEN YOU ARE WEAK AND LOSE YOUR FOCUS, IT WILL EASILY DEFEAT YOU.

In *Exodus 17:8-16*, we read that when the people of Israel were on the way to the Promised Land, Amalek goes out to meet them and in a cowardly manner attacks them from the rear. Amalek attacked the weak and discouraged and ravaged them from behind. This is exactly what happens in some Christian congregations when it's only a few who are given over to prayer and intercession. So then, what happens to those that stay behind? Sometimes they are walking slowly and distracted. Amalek attacks those that are lagging behind and are losing sight of the vision. They that stay behind spiritually are on a dangerous position: they become a target for the enemy.

If you are feeling discouraged and have allowed others to take over and take care of things, if you are feeling frustrated over attitudes of the past due to hurts, I'll tell you something: Don't stay in a place of indifference. Move forward!!! Get to the front of the battle and overcome in the name of Jesus! Do it as a prophetic act in these last days! Those that are in the front lines are going to be the ones to have a clearer vision and will be able to participate in the great victories for the Kingdom.

Begin With the Visible Battles

As Israel approached Raphidim, they were met by Amalek's surprise attack, whose purpose was to demolish them. In this we can see the spirit that was involved in the battle, because they had bitterness and hate against the people of God. This war continues even today.

When there is a divine destiny before you, the spirit of Amalek will always rise to hold you back with opposition. Its purpose will be to:

- Detain you.
- Abort God's plans for you.
- Keep you distracted in the desert.
- Avoid your entering in and enjoying the blessing of God's abundant provision.

The word Rediphim means "space" or "hold" (a place of rest). Moses went up to mount Rediphim; it is here where the soul, weary under the pressures of spiritual battles, receives direct support from heaven and from the Holy Spirit. This is the same support that was received by Moses, Hur and Aaron. Moses quickly dispatches instructions on how to proceed:

So Moses said to Joshua, "Choose men for us and go out, fight against Amalek tomorrow; I will station myself on the top of the hill with the staff of God in my hand." Exodus 17:9

Moses was also a man of great courage, but he also had faithful persons around him who supported his vision in covenant. Aaron and Hur supported him with intercession.

WHEN YOU FEEL ANNOYED AND UNDER PRESSURE, DO NOT STAY ALONE. TEMPTATIONS WILL SURELY COME AND IT WILL BE EASY FOR THE ENEMY TO DEFEAT YOU.

Moses' strategy was to have unity in teamwork. Pray with someone to strengthen your inner man, God is glorified when there is unity and two can come together in agreement.

If you decide to serve God in order to be an overcomer, make a covenant with him.

You need to know that anything that is not under the covenant is illegal. Every illegal relationship outside of God's designs do not lead to blessing, they lead to curses. This is why man needs to enter in the "new covenant", established with the blood of Jesus in order to receive the blessing of His grace.

As long as Moses held up his hands, the Israelites were winning, but whenever he lowered his hands, the Amalekites were winning. Exodus17:11

This means that you're in a battle in which you need to get God's approval. It is written that the Lord will fight against Amalek from generation to generation. This means that the struggle against Amalek will be a daily one as long as you remain on earth. When you make a decision to take up the challenges with God, Amalek is going to chase after you. From the moment that you cease to live by the Spirit and love God intimately, Amalek begins to gain strength. *When Moses' hands grew tired, [...] Aaron and Hur held his hands up—one on one side, one on the other... Exodus 17:12*

It is unfortunate that today when someone's hands grow tired, there are others ready to knock him down. **The secret of unity is essential to gaining complete victory.**

▓ *The Secret to Being Connected*

Joshua was united to is spiritual authority; Moses, and in turn, Moses was united to a supernatural authority, who was God Himself. *In order to defeat Amalek, you need to be connected to your pastor and hold his hands up high*, for when they are above, some hidden Amalek lying below, fighting against your fallen nature, will not be able to demolish you. Joshua's name was *Yeshua*, which in Hebrew means "God of my salvation" and "Jesus". What does this mean? That Joshua was a type and shadow of Jesus. He was always connected to His leader. If Jesus had not been connected to His Heavenly Father, He would have never been able to defeat evil. And here is the secret, teamwork.

THAT WHICH GAVE JESUS THE POWER AND ABILITY TO TRIUMPH, WAS HIS RELATIONSHIP OF HONOR AND RESPECT TOWARDS THE ONE ABOVE HIM. HE NEVER LOOSED HIMSELF FROM THE FEAR OF GOD. REVERENCE AND RESPECT WERE HIS STRENGTH.

You need to be connected to a spiritual authority. You cannot walk alone through life. God reveals Himself as the God who is your helper. The only one who can free you from the slavery of the flesh is His Son, Jesus Christ, there is no other. The only thing you can do is to cry out and seek union with people of God who are under authority. *The most powerful strategy to go forward is unity*. Amalek was way too strong and astute. Don't ever stray from your brethren in the faith, nor stay isolated in front of the battle. It is only the powerful weapon of unity that can take advantage over the enemy.

Thus, Joshua was courageous, Moses was the interceding prophet, Aaron represented the priesthood and Hur was the man of faith, who was in partnership with Aaron in the governing of the people by Mount Sinai.

Having the Same Vision as Your Leader

As long as you want to be close to your pastors, the devil will set his eyes on you to separate you and attack you. When you decide to remain firm, face to face, pushing forth God's purposes, don't forget that Amalek will be working to disrupt you and pull you away from the vision. However, think on this: If you are fighting the good fight of faith, and "Moses", your spiritual leader, is close by crying out to God for your life, I assure you Amalek will not be able to defeat you.

While Davis was in Galaad, the Amalekites forged a surprise attack on him in the camp at Ziklag. Amalek always attacks legal authority. It attacks with thoughts and comments such as: "I don't agree with the pastor, I love him, but I don't agree with what he does or his vision." It doesn't matter what position you have in the church, you are definitively being attacked by the spirit that wants to disconnect you from the body of Christ and the vision. God told Davis to take back everything that Amalek had stolen from him, (see *1 Samuel 30*). Here Amalek represents the worldly spirit, the love of money, philosophies of man such as humanism, liberalism, post modernism and **that whole collection of philosophies that exalt man and replace him for the Creator and Lord over all**.

This is then a spirit of lies and arrogance against the Almighty God. Why then, does God enter into battle with Amalek from generation to generation? Because Amalek tempts you to do things which you should not do, and God says to you "Be done with Amalek!!"

And this is precisely Amalek's purpose: to attack spiritual authority. If you say that God has revealed something to you, but it is not in agreement with the vision that God has given the house where you serve, something isn't working right. God is a God of order. First God has to reveal it to the house pastor. The reason Joshua was able to defeat Amalek is because he was connected to Moses.

If God is at war with Amalek, we are also at war against him. We need to have a leadership that moves in the power, Word and revelation of God, and that does not compromise with sin. Do not stay behind mired in the desert; go instead to the land where there is the power, glory and authority that God has for you.

6

REACH SUCCESS IN THE MIDST OF PRESSURES

...because heaving will be on your side

Sometimes a victory isn't attained because of ignorance regarding the facts of the battle.

Amalek was ready, they were headed for war. Israel was marching towards a promise and had no inclination towards battling. Many today fail in their spiritual life because they have no idea that to accept Christ is to enter into battle. Paul calls it "contending for the faith."

Let us look at the details concerning Moses in the desert. *"So Moses said to Joshua, "Choose men for us* (he didn't say "warriors," no, he said "men") *and go out, fight against Amalek. Tomorrow I will station myself on the top of the hill with the staff of God in my hand." Exodus 17:9* The people of Israel were not warriors, nor were they ready for this. Let us keep in mind that they lasted more than four hundred years oppressed in slavery to Pharaoh's empire. None of them had any training to go into battle. Slaves were trained only to be used for service under the oppressor's yoke. Therefore, they lacked the capability to confront Amalek and his fierce warriors. Israel depended on God completely.

There are many people who are set free from the slavery of the flesh, but when they begin the Christian walk, they become passive in their spiritual life. Jesus Christ has washed and cleansed them with His blood, but they have no understanding of spiritual warfare. They have spent their whole lives tied to an oppressor who has kept them trapped in a road to complete destruction. When all of a sudden God appears in their life, they receive the forgiveness for their sins and are cleansed, but when they need to face a battle with their own flesh, they don't know how to obtain victory. They do not know and no one has explained to them that when someone is converted to Christ, all of hell begins to declare war on them.

Awareness in Spiritual Battle

Joshua never questioned Moses why he was giving orders. He never complained nor argued. Joshua only obeyed orders because he knew his leader and respected him.

LEADERS IN THE FRONTLINES KNOW HOW TO FIND THEIR PLACE TO ACCEPT WHATEVER GOD IS TELLING THEM.

The Bible says that Joshua obeyed the mandate that Moses gave him: *"Joshua did as Moses told him," Exodus 17:10* Joshua knew that the people were not ready for battle and that the Lord would overcome their enemies. As the strategy, Moses says: *"Tomorrow I will station myself on the top of the hill with the staff of God in my hand." Exodus 17:9* The very first question that could have sparked in Joshua's or anyone else's mind was; "So what is Moses doing on top of the hill?" Alternatively, "Why is he leaving us alone in this very crucial time of the battle?" Yet, that is not what Joshua thought.

The Bible says: *"But the natural man does not receive the things of the Spirit of God, for they are foolishness to him; nor can he know them, because they are spiritually discerned." 1 Corinthians 2:14* the natural mind will never comprehend what God is doing.

The staff in Moses was carrying represents the divine authority given to him by God. Therefore, he would have the decision making power in his hands. Moses and Joshua accepted the challenge. God's logic was not for Moses to go into battle face to face with the Amalekites, but for him to be on top of the hill. Now, God did not always accomplish things in Israel's wars the in same way as on this occasion. He doesn't have to limit Himself to doing things the same, for He is able do anything as He desires.

It was not for Moses to stay down in the plain, but rather he was to go up to the hill where he would join God in a direct, one on one relationship. Then, when Moses would raise his hands, God would connect with him. Thus, Moses would become an intermediary in the battle between Amalek and the Almighty God. He was a bridge between the human and the divine, between the earthly and the powerful, victory and failure, between what God pours and what He's about to do on earth. This was an act of obedience, and when we do likewise, the glory of God envelopes us. If you raise your hands without knowledge or revelation, nothing happens, but if you do it depending totally on His grace and favor, you will be more than a conqueror.

Moses' hands grew weary, if they had not, the battle would have been shorter. But he did get tired. It was at this point, that Aaron and Hur had an idea: they took a stone and sat him upon it. A rock remains unchanged in its place. This is a type and shadow of Jesus. As long as you are seated upon the foundations of your own nature, Amalek will overcome you.

WHEN YOU ARE SEATED ON THE FIRM CORNERSTONE, WHICH IS JESUS CHRIST, THERE IS NOTHING THAT CAN MOVE YOU OFF BASE, FOR YOU ARE FIRMLY ESTABLISHED UPON AN UNSHAKEABLE ROCK.

Although Moses sat on the stone because he was surely tired, what Aaron and Hur did was a prophetic act. Physical as well as spiritual battles are hard. Even though Moses was seated, the actual struggle was taking place in his hands, but they continued to hold his hands up. One of the most difficult battles that a pastor or minister has to endure is solitude. Even when surrounded by people and a loving church, there are many tears cried before God over being alone. And yet, Aaron and Hur were right there, people of prayer who were by his side and helped to uphold him. In this war against Amalek, join forces with the people of God, driven by prayer and who live in a greater spiritual level. Don't join those who are highly opinionated and talk too much. Don't draw close to those who are empty, or to those who have never helped to restore anyone, who have never cared to cast out a demon, to not leave someone oppressed. Stay away from those who have never bothered to pray for healing and deliverance of someone else in the name of Jesus.

There are times when you alone will obtain the victory, but there are other times when you will experience a corporate victory. In the majority of cases, you will need the help of others to break off what Amalek has against you. If the devil knows that he can make you lose a battle, then he already considers you a loser. When Amalek was crushed and vanquished, Israel's fame spread to the rest of the world. When the devil realizes that he can no longer play with your mind or your emotions, because you have perfect communion with God and you are surrendered completely to Him, I assure you that the devil will tremble because he knows you are a person who is destined for victory.

You need to obey God in everything that He tells you. The point is not to help God out, but to do as He says. There are certain battles that you can win in a matter of hours, but there are others that take years. Do you know why? Because everything depends on your attitude of obedience towards God, and if this is not happening, it is better that you ask yourself why you are not reaching the victory. Where is the flaw? The key is that the battle is His, not ours. You need to rise above the obstacles; circumstances and barriers achieve the purposes that God has declared to you.

All Moses had to do was raise his hands; his part was to intercede for the people. Hur and Aaron's part was to lift Moses' hands, but not in the same spot, one was to the right and the other to the left. Remember than throughout all of this, there was a strategy and the mission had to be fulfilled in the manner that God had shown. In each move of God, He wants to use us in a different manner.

Who Defeats Amalek?

PEOPLE AFTER GOD'S OWN HEART. David was a man after God's own heart. That is why when the Amalekite came to give him the news that he had killed King Saul, he felt no joy, since the Amalekites as a people were the enemies of God. King David could not have rejoiced over such an event. This is why we should never accept nor feel any pleasure when the works of Satan has harmed a brother in the faith, no matter what the condition of that person at the time.

The only people for whom it is possible to destroy Amalek are those who are after God's own heart. Amalek is a spirit with delegated authority to confuse and destroy. We will not be able to destroy our internal and external Amaleks if in our hearts we are not seeking God's heart. The very first thing we need to do is to surrender our heart and all its attitudes to God. The Bible says that the mouth speaks out of the abundance of the heart, and the evil that comes from man is not in what he eats, but rather what comes out of his mouth. It's what is within the heart that counts.

The price that Saul paid was not his throne or his life, but the lives of his sons. If you do not take spiritual authority over the things to which God has declared war, they will destroy you. You cannot join forces and agree with what offends God, because if you do, you become His enemy.

Worship God in the Midst of Trials

The tribe of Judah is a type of praise and worship. Simeon, as the name indicates in Hebrew, means "to hear or to be listening," which is equivalent to the anointing for intercession that is needed to enter into spiritual warfare. The lesson here is that in order to enter into war with Amalek, you need to develop a deep level of praise, worship and intercession. To completely demolish this spirit it is necessary for you to fill yourself with praises, worship, thanksgiving, and to decide that no matter what, you will say the same as the prophet *in Habakkuk 3:17-18: "Though the fig tree should not blossom, and there be no fruit on the vines, Though the yield of the olive should fail, and the fields produce no food, although the flock should be cut off from the fold, and there be no cattle in the stalls, yet I will exult in the Lord, I will rejoice in the God of my salvation."*

This is the decisive factor in the plan of victory against Amalek. This spirit will try to get your life to where you will begin to murmur and complain, criticize and be disposed towards all kinds of negativity. Turn the dynamic around, use praise as a crucial weapon against Amalek. Keep in mind that the devil will be screaming at you: "You can't be worshipping God! Why the financial crisis is worsening and your finances are going down-hill, the pain is overwhelming you and your marriage is only getting worse!" But even so, tell the Lord, "Father, even though I walk through the valley of darkness and death, I will not fear what the enemy can do to me, because your rod and your staff comfort me, you prepare a table for me in front of my enemies, surely goodness and mercy will follow me all the days of my life and I will live in the house of the Lord forever."

When you begin to worship God, you enter into Amalek's territory and you can cast him out. But first, you must worship God and then you can use intercessory prayer and war. An intercessor must be a powerful worshipper, because the two go hand in hand.

7

GET TO KNOW
AMALEK

...so you can defeat him

Amalek Represents Unregenrate Man

Amalek is the sin that man carries as a result of our fallen nature. Paul refers to this condition as "the flesh." In the book of Galatians 5:19-21 it is expressed this way: *"Now the deeds of the flesh are evident, which are: immorality, impurity, sensuality, idolatry, sorcery, enmities, strife, jealousy, outbursts of anger, disputes, dissensions, factions, envying, drunkenness, carousing, and things like these, of which I forewarn you, just as I have forewarned you, that those who practice such things will not inherit the kingdom of God."*

Here we see how Amalek represents the works of the flesh, which are conceived and carried out in the heart and mind. All of the conflicts that war against the soul have its origins in the fall of nature.

Many of these traits are inherited from one generation to the next.

However, many others are just a result of the lustful desires that stem from man's fallen nature, which are conceived in the heart and are outwardly manifested by disobedience to God's commandments.

James clarifies the condition further when he tells us: *But each one is tempted when he is carried away and enticed by his own lust* (sinful desires). *Then when lust has conceived, it gives birth to sin; and when sin is accomplished,* (the complete cycle) *it brings forth death.* What great depths in this paragraph of Scripture! This is where the evil residing in the heart of man hides. Each and every believer who sets himself on the road to conquer his destiny in God will encounter this most powerful and dangerous enemy; his very own nature. This is the most significant area of conflict, which rises up against the purposes that God has for the new believer.

Romans 7:17-21 says: So now, no longer am I the one doing it, but sin which dwells in me. For I know that nothing good dwells in me, that is, in my flesh; for the willing is present in me, but the doing of the good is not. For the good that I want, I do not do, but I practice the very evil that I do not want. But if I am doing the very thing I do not want, I am no longer the one doing it, but sin which dwells in me. I find then the principle that evil is present in me, the one who wants to do good.

When your very own flesh rises up against you, it does so in order to detain your destiny. It will always try to drag you into discouragement and despair. In your thoughts, you remember your failures and you can feel outside pressures from family members and adverse circumstances. We call this battle "the flesh" or the "old self." It is from this premise, that we are presenting this chapter as Amalek's treason. Amalek will always rise up from deep within you and its roots are derived from the same rebellion and persecution as your fallen nature. The purpose is to deviate you from your walk with Christ and to get you to where you are a defeated Christian.

Do you know why it is that you do that which you do not wish to do? Because Amalek was woven into the fabric of each human being. Your flesh will never be able to get rid of him, but you can live with him overcome and under your feet daily. One thing that can help in prevent problems is to avoid bad company that can confuse you and drag you into sin. Even when you consider yourself "mature" and you think that you are above anyone teaching you anything, your flesh will still be persecuting you night and day inside of you.

■ *Why do You feel Overcome by Temptations?*

The answer is in the book of *Deuteronomy 245:17-19 Remember what Amalek did to you along the way when you came out from Egypt, how he met you along the way and attacked among you all the stragglers at your rear when you were faint and weary; and he did not fear God. Therefore it shall come about when the LORD your God has given you rest from all your surrounding enemies, in the land which the LORD your God gives you as an inheritance to possess, you shall blot out the memory of Amalek from under heaven; you must not forget.*

Amalek always comes from the rearguard and attacks from behind; it operates like a spirit of retaliation. Sometimes you will even feel oppression on your back, as if you were carrying a

100-pound load. You will feel pain and exhaustion. Remember this: Amalek is fighting you from behind; it is a spirit of vengeance that takes advantage of you when you are feeling weak in the faith and distracted.

There are times when you are unknowingly allowing your own soul to be subject to bondage, by allowing yourself to look into something forbidden or that has an adverse effect spiritually. It usually happens during the most insignificant instances of daily living; such as an out of line remark, a moment of anger, a bad attitude, that your "old self" comes out again. If you feel like you are tired spiritually, remember Matthew 11:28, Jesus says; "come to Me and I will give you rest." Also, keep in mind that the Word says in Joel 3:10; "Let the weak say 'I am strong'." And you need to be strong, because if you give in your flesh causes you to fall in defeat. This is why Paul explains clearly in Galatians 5:16-17 *But I say, walk by the Spirit, and you will not carry out the desire of the flesh. For the flesh sets its desire against the Spirit, and the Spirit against the flesh; for these are in opposition to one another, so that you may not do the things that you please.*

> THE SPIRIT OF GOD AND THE SPIRIT OF FLESH WILL BE IN CONFLICT FROM GENERATION TO GENERATION.
>
> **Jehovah-Nissi is your banner.**

The most crucial moment in the battle between Joshua and Amalek, was the end, for this victory was won with the Lord's sword. You must never forget that the Spirit of the Lord is in His Word, that powerful weapon which crushes Amalek and his followers. Moses built an altar with the name Jehovah-Nissi, in remembrance of this victory, but at the same time he declared that from this day forth there would always be a war against Amalek, asserting: *"... and he said, "The LORD has sworn; the LORD will have war against Amalek from generation to generation." Exodus 17:16*

When Evil Thoughts Attack You

And do you know who is really being attacked? Even though it is indirect, it is an attack against the body of Christ as a whole, which is the church. This is the reason why God Himself will fight for you. When your thoughts are at war with Amalek, subjugate and conquer! When you feel alone and walking through a desert, crush him! Amalek comes against everything that belongs to God. If you are one of His chosen treasures, do not walk away from His protection. Hide in His presence, for that is the only place where you will be safe. The greater the pressures in your life, the closer you need to be to God. Perhaps you are saying: "but, I can't feel Him." It doesn't matter, He is right there. Even though you may not see or hear Him, by faith He is right there to help you. Every time you win a struggle against your own flesh, the Lord will be lifting a banner (Jehovah-Nissi) over your life. The Word says in *Isaiah 59:19: When the enemy shall come in like a flood, the Spirit of the Lord shall lift up a standard against him.* Remember that the standard, or banner, is the sign that He places over your life in the spiritual world to show that you are an overcomer. He gives you power and authority. No matter what comes your way, whether he tries to discourage, confuse, detain, attack you and your blessings from God or your finances, Jehovah-Nissi will lift up a standard of victory, and you can rest beneath its shadow.

When Amalek is defeated, the standard of Jehovah-Nissi is raised.

A standard is a banner that represents a nation or kingdom and is used to identify it. When you are able to defeat your own Amalek, or your negative thoughts and actions, God installs His own banner. Amalek is a clever spirit that disguises itself in order to make you miss your purpose in God. He wants you to lose focus and perspective from the designs that Almighty God has for you. This is the reason why frequently, when there are internal wars, conflicts and crisis brewing in a church congregation, Amalek is working behind the scene. A spirit of insubordination does not respect delegated authority, not even the ones placed by God. It always tries to create and impose its own authority and it is cunning and manipulative. It also works to weaken passions and desires for the Lord's fire, causing you to become bland and lukewarm. There are people who will shed tears over another person, but never for the presence of God in their lives.

Yet, always keep this in mind: If Jehovah-Nissi plants a banner and sets up a standard; there is no Amalek that can touch or topple you. You shall have power over your finances and marriage. You will not give up and you will rise up like a courageous soldier to destroy whatever force tries to come against you.

How the Flesh is Overcome

Only the death of Jesus on the cross was able to defeat our most ferocious enemy; the old, unregenerate flesh. **YOU** and **I**, have to go to the cross to die over and over again, so that we might be raised with Christ. Jesus Christ, the last Adam, won the victory for all humanity, but only those that believe in Him can apply this for themselves.

This is why our victory over Amalek consists in depending on Jesus Christ and His redemptive work. No one can be free without first going to Calvary, taking up their cross and following the Master. When you pray, do it in this manner: **"You spirit of vengeance, I bind and rebuke you and I forbid you to manifest. I know your name; Amalek, and right now in the name of Jesus Christ, I forbid you to come against me, my home, my family, my finances and my life. You will not be able to hold me back, for I have decided to reach all of the plans and purposes that God has assigned for me. I am more than a conqueror in His powerful and eternal name."**

8

THE RESURGENCE OF AGAG

...throughout the generations

Amalek, King of the Amalekites

Agag lived around the same time as King Saul. He was the king of the Amalekites, who lived south of Israel. The name 'Agag' means, "I will stand out." Although he was a prince and head of the Agagites, he had Amalekite blood. There was a prophecy that still had not come to pass, for God does not forget what He foretells. After the battle at Rediphim, led by Moses and Joshua, God spoke about the complete destruction of the enemies of God who persecuted His people. As the prophecy stated that the first king would destroy Amalek, it would be precisely fulfilled in Saul. It would be his charge to execute vengeance over Israel's staunchest enemies.

Time for reflection: if God has told you to do

something, it is best you do it quickly. The enemy will try in every way possible to detain you from accomplishing the original purpose of paramount importance for which God chose you.

SOMETIMES TIMING IS OF SUCH CONSEQUENCE, THAT IF YOU LOSE THE MOMENT YOU LOSE THE OPPORTUNITY.

Agag represented "hate incarnate against divine purposes," the persistence of hatred and resentment throughout the generations. At that time, Agag represented the Amalekites and the prophet Samuel represented the purity, the presence and the rule of God. Here we find the juxtaposition between darkness and light, hate as opposed to love, and disobedience against righteousness against truth and justice.

Samuel crowns Saul, not by God's orders, but by the petition of the people. Even so, God reminds Saul of the prophecy that is still to be fulfilled regarding the first king of Israel. He says to him: *"Now go and strike Amalek and utterly destroy all that he has, and do not spare him; but put to death both man and woman, child and infant, ox and sheep, camel and donkey." 1 Samuel 15:3*

Yet, Saul does not obey God's instructions word by word. He left Agag, his wife, and fattened animals alive, and some of their belongings. Therefore, the prophet Samuel came to him and rebuked him for his misdeeds, and told him, among other things, that he was small before his eyes, (since he was from the tribe of Benjamin, one of the most insignificant), and now the Lord had anointed him as king over Israel.

God had a purpose in choosing Saul from one of the smallest tribes. Of course He could have chosen him from the tribe of Judah, and yet, that is not how God chose to do it. Perhaps He did it so that in the future this king would not become arrogant, nor become exalted in his own heart.

Samuel reminds him: *"Is it not true, though you were little in your own eyes, you were made the head of the tribes of Israel? And the Lord anointed you king over Israel." 1 Samuel 15:17* So then, why was he anointed king? So that he could not make up new orders that were not spoken by the mouth of God or the prophet. *"Why then did you not obey the voice of the Lord, but rushed upon the spoil and did what was evil in the sight of the Lord?" 1 Samuel 15:19*

Saul's sin was that he considered himself too wise and shrewd to heed the prophet's orders. Saul's thoughts were different from the mind of God. He reasoned that the animals were good for use as sacrificial offerings at the temple's altar. Instead of killing them as he was told, he figured that they were too good to not keep alive. Thus, he simply followed a human line of thinking and did not follow rules. No idea, no matter how good it may seem, if not in line with God's thinking, is a good idea.

SOME IDEOLOGIES HAVE BEEN PASSED ON SO AS TO CONTRADICT DIVINE PRINCIPLES.

Analyze your ideas, because they do not always line up with heaven.

God gave an order, and He said: *"Thus says the Lord of hosts, 'I will punish Amalek for what he did to Israel, how he set himself against him on the way while he was coming up from Egypt.'* (to the promised land) *1 Samuel 15:2* God had not forgotten that he gives the order to Saul and says:

"Now go and strike Amalek and utterly destroy all that he has, and do not spare him; but put to death both man and woman, child and infant, ox and sheep, camel and donkey." 1 Samuel 15:3

Do you see it? The command was: "Everything that comes from Amalek must be destroyed." Saul fought against Amalek and his people, but because he gave a truce, he ended up being killed by an Amalekite. He neither obeyed nor lined up with the prophecy, therefore he lost the opportunity to become a part of the divine plan.

Many live under the pressure of their own opinions and have an erroneous idea about God. An ideology borne from the human imagination is not the plan of God, and does not have God's perfect structure.

How can one understand what is God's plan and what s not? To better understand, we could put it something like this: A lie is like one of Amalek's small child. A forbidden look is like one of his daughters. There are things that may seem very small, but in reality, they are the product of wrong thinking and an erroneous mind, like Saul's. If you allow "little things" (which are the vain imaginations without any structure from the Word of God) to grow and develop in your life, they will become a spirit that will dominate you and you will reach a point where you will be unable to get rid of the effects.

If you do not declare war on Amalek, he will end up preventing your arrival to the land of provision and success. You must overcome him while you are still in the desert. If not, when you are alone in your trials and he is persecuting and warring with you, he will have the power over you that he would not have, had you entered into the promised land.

When you have no knowledge of the plans that God has for your life, Amalek has the supremacy over your destiny. However, when you know who you are in Christ and what God thinks and says about you, there goes the end of Amalek's dominion over you. Saul had two kinds of confrontations, Amalek on the inside and Agag on the outside. The fact is, he was unable to defeat the enemy on the inside because he had been unable to overcome the one on the outside.

If you are unable to overcome your enemies on the inside, you will be unable to overcome the ones that attack you on the outside. It is imperative that you take your power and authority to defeat from the top down all of the things that are attempting to wrecking havoc and destruction within you. Included in this list are: anger, rage, resentment, grudges, quarrels, hate, conflicts, disrespect, a root of bitterness, rejection, low self-esteem, gossip, hate, fleshly pleasures, lust, adultery, fornication, lies, idolatry, consulting the occult, curiosity into the forbidden by God, etc. You must be able to effectively rid yourself of your inner attackers before you can go on to challenge your external ones.

After Saul pardoned Agag's life, he went to commit another act of foolishness. He raised a monument, a great pillar, in his own honor. The raising of this boastful trophy was an additional step of disobedience, as his arrogance had taken the place of his sense of duty. This was a symbol of his exulting of his own human power and the desire to do and undo things according to his own whims, and not taking God's desires into consideration.

IT IS LIKE TAKING HOLD OF A FALSE SENSE OF FREEDOM, WHICH GIVES YOU THE RIGHT TO MAKE YOUR OWN

DECISIONS.

On the very night of this memorable occasion to Saul's "pride," God reveals Himself to Samuel and says: *"I regret that I have made Saul king, for he has turned back from following Me and has not carried out My commands " And Samuel was distressed and cried out to the Lord all night. [...] For rebellion is as the sin of divination, and insubordination is as iniquity and idolatry, because you have rejected the word of the Lord, He has also rejected you from being king." 1 Samuel 15:11, 23*

"I regret," what God said, is just as if saying; "I feel remorse over Saul," and from then on the Lord departed from him.

DISOBEDIENCE AND SELF-ADORATION IS A SIN BEGUN BY SATAN. THIS INNER PRIDE MIXED WITH OCCULTISM SEPARATES FROM GOD'S TRANSPARENT COMMUNICATION.

Saul's spirit, the same as the spirit of hidden resentment, does not heed God's commandments and resists obedience to the established Word. To feel more important than God and not depend on

His Word, is close to not needing Him at all. This makes the Spirit that lives within us to become grieved and far from us.

How to Overcome Our Agagites

The prophetic anointing over Samuel was visible; it gave him authority and righteousness. Saul represented the natural man, in a hurry and full of anxiety, who has no idea how to wait on God and obey His will. Saul was used to hearing God through Samuel. Samuel was like a mentor to him, but there comes a time in the spiritual life of every person when he has to mature, in the same way that a son who takes up his responsibilities and leaves home to get married.

Saul insisted upon disobeying and making hurried decisions instead of consulting with God. He thought that his "calling" gave him absolute authority to decide and act on his own. It must not be forgotten that the authority inherent in occupying a certain position must always be accompanied by submission to a higher authority. Without submission, there is authority without any backing. God operates through teamwork. Saul was supposed to work in unison with the prophet. So

147

many Christians today are used to making decisions independent from God! Not all decisions are made in God; because usually the time is not taken to make sure that ultimate decisions are in accordance with God's will.

Agag represents hatred, and only by eliminating it and substituting it with love, will there be any success in changing this in your generation. Only the prophetic anointing, like what Samuel had, can uproot it effectively. If in your generation there are family divisions, divorces, resentments and grudges, enmity between in-laws, parents against children, etc., there is a three-cord strand stronghold that must be broken.

IF WE DO NOT EFFECTIVELY CUT THE INFLUENCE OF THE GENERATIONAL SPIRITS PASSED DOWN FROM OUR ANCESTORS, THESE WILL TAKE GREATER STRENGTH IN THE NEXT GENERATION.

God is raising up a prophetic generation that will declare judgment against Amalek and Agag, who are the spirits assigned against this generation.

9

THE POWER OF THE SIGNET RING

...gives you the authority to change the law

The seed of the curse of Agag remained alive inside the womb of his wife. When she fled to distant lands, she took it with her. It was that evil inheritance from Amalek that was growing in secret once again, able to pass on from generation to generation. In due time she gave birth to a male, and out of the vast Persian Empire came Haman, a direct descendant of Agag, hence, an Amalekite. The name Haman in Hebrew means "magnificent." He was the son of Hammedatha (Persian name) an Agagite (we find the story in *Esther 3:1, 10; 8:3, 5; 9:24*) and high official in the court of King Ahasuerus, also called Xerxes. Josephus the historian asserts in one of his writings that he was a relative of the royal house of the Amalekites. This relationship might explain the deep hatred that Haman felt towards the Jews and his desire to utterly destroy them. This was not limited to his personal enemy, Mordecai, but included the entire nation that had been the archenemy of his ancestors' people.

As a favorite of King Xerxes, Haman was very annoyed and frustrated that Mordecai refused to give him the honor and adulation he felt he deserved. Therefore, he made plans to destroy all of the Jews. For this, he would need to occupy a higher position and enjoy the king's favor.

The Idolatrous Image

Haman had embroidery placed on his garments that not only identified him with his ancestors, the Amalekites, but with his ideal. For a very long time he had been scheming a sinister plan in his heart, and the time was getting close for him to be able to fulfill his wicked desires. All of those who would lie prostrate before him were also reverencing the image unawares. This design was an unquestionable representation of his rank and the increase of generational power. This is exactly how the enemy of mankind has operated undetected for centuries. He has always identified with secret signs, symbols, and signals, and often by means of handshakes and gestures. Only those who have been through initiation rites into secret brotherhoods and fraternities can recognize these.

The Power of Ambition and Arrogance

In the heart of Haman, the Agagite there was a generational hatred towards the people of God. Now we can see clearly how this spirit of hatred moved from generation to generation. Once he reached a position of power, given to him by the Persian king, his resentment begins to manifest. Haman was raised as a prince, who could have access to see the king face to face, that is to say, that he could be with the king in his very own palace. This position afforded him the privilege of being one of the seven most important princes in Ahasuerus' kingdom.

HAMAN IS AN EXAMPLE OF A MAN WHO WIL DOES THE UNTHINKABLE TO GET TO A HIGH SOCIAL STANDING OF POWER, AND ALL THAT WILL GENERATE WEALTH.

The two secret plans.

Remember that the very first sin in the universe

153

was that of pride in Lucifer the angel, who wanted to be god, he coveted power and worshipped himself.

Haman had two great plans. One was to exterminate all of the Jewish people of the empire, and the second was that every person would have to bow before him when he walked through the city. Now, not happy with that, he wanted that whenever he was to pass mounted on his horse, all would make a show of reverence. Pride became enmeshed with arrogance and power.

God resists pride and self-promotion: *"God resists the proud, but gives grace to the humble." James 4:6*

Mordecai, faithful in his knowledge of the Law of Moses, refuses to bow before Haman, in spite of this being a law sealed by the very ring of King Ahasuerus (also known as Xerxes).

The spirit of hatred will always try to humiliate others. Every time you do something good in God's eyes, but in your mind you feel like you are being bombarded by accusations, understand that there is an Agagite spirit that is chasing after you.

This is the spirit of Haman who hates God's generation. It does not matter if it is a relative, a mother or a father who has cursed you and accused you always. It is not really the person, but a spirit sent to persecute you. In the same manner, just as we specified in the beginning of this book, the pressures of racial hatred is all over the world. Racial and ethnic hatred and divisions become more and more firmly rooted with the passage of time. People feel insecure with their governments and in their cities and towns, as if they have been left without protection. Many today are living in constant discouragement, loneliness and confusion.

Therefore, today more than ever we need to be firmly established in our faith, for there are storms that come in the direction of our trust and emotional stability. The days of Haman draw closer. Haman represents the usurped authority inside of governments that makes the minds of those in charge to be controlled and manipulated by these spirits of oppression. If we actually had firm individuals like Mordecai, we would be able to change the direction of governing bodies. Mordecai counsels, encourages and struggles to establish God's law in a place that was far from his native land, where neither his laws nor his culture applies. Therefore, always give the glory to your Savior, and heaven will protect you.

In a world where the laws are contrary to God's laws, many Christians today more than ever, find themselves grappling against ideologies contrary to what God teaches in His Word.

Haman's Conspiracy

Haman, the enemy of all the Jews, had come up with an idea for their complete annihilation. To bring this about, he was counting on the king's signet ring, which would provide the stamp of authority that the order required. The seal was the guarantee that his plans would go forward. (See *Esther 3:8-13*) A decree was a very important order. To bring it into present day terms, it would be like revoking a law by means of an amendment. This procedure takes time. In the Persian Empire, no one could stand in opposition to a decree sealed by the king. In verse 3:10, it says that, *"Then the king took his signet ring from his hand and gave it to Haman, the son of Hammedatha the Agagite, the enemy of the Jews."*

Haman decided to trust in the lot that was cast on the first day of the year. The word "pur," means "luck," according to the Babylonian religion at the time, when people believed that the gods gathered on the first day of the year to cast lots that would determine the fate of each person. We must never forget that God is above every human decree. In *Proverbs 16:33* it says that the final decision in all of man's affairs is at the hand of God. *"The lot is cast into the lap, but its every decision is from the Lord."*

It is not luck that controls destiny in the lives of mankind, but the sovereignty of God.

In this day and age, human laws plague the minds of Christians and many think that they are pleasing God by conforming to them. This vivid example shows us that God's laws are to be obeyed above man's laws. Although God has indeed given power to rulers and all authority is given by Him, the Word of God also says that He honors those who honor Him.

The Jews were dispersed among the many cities of the great empire. The Persian Empire spanned across part of the civilized world from the year 553 AC to 331AC. In spite of their being widely spread out, they did not adopt the customs or the culture, and they certainly could not come into opposition over the king's decrees. Now, Mordecai and Esther did in fact integrate into Persian society. Mordecai was one of the scribes in the king's palace. *Foreigners today should become part of the society where they are living, as long as they do not compromise their Christian principles.*

The decree established under the power of the signet ring.

The royal seal for the Persian Empire in those days was used to close letters and other documents with a resinous substance. Persons in public administration would stamp their own, personal symbol, usually engraved on a ring, upon the soft, warm substance, giving a character of importance to the sealed paper. We can thus understand, how very important the power of a signet is, and how dangerous should the sealed papers fall into the wrong hands. Haman knew the power of possessing the king's ring. Once he would have access to it, it would facilitate his ambition to decree the laws that for a very long time he had been maliciously planning.

These decrees had been devised in his favor, even if they were against the law of God. His plan would allow him to climb higher in power and position. The Bible tells us in *Esther 3:10 "Then the king took his signet ring from his hand and gave it to Haman, the son of Hammedatha the Agagite, the enemy of the Jews."*

Spiritually, Haman represents the inheritance of the spirit of hate. He was finally able to reach a position of authority from where he could enact and carry out laws that would exterminate an entire race. Once he was able to obtain through "legal channels" the power to implement his malignant plan, he decrees a death sentence for every Jew living within the limits of the territorial extension of the Medo-Persian Empire. *Letters were sent by couriers to all the king's provinces to destroy, to kill and to annihilate all the Jews, both young and old, women and children, in one day, (...), and to seize their possessions as plunder. Esther3:13*

How often does power fall into the wrong hands? How often are laws dictated to us from corrupt individuals? How many trials have ended in the sentencing of those who are innocent? Sometimes the authority to implement certain laws is in the hands of those whose minds are oppressed by various ethnic prejudices. Under these circumstances, justice degrades into the harassment of innocents.

The seal is a way of communicating closure and approval to a decree. The word *decree* means: rule. Command, judgment, edict, fiat, order, precept. In Haman's case, the decree was completely broken by divine intervention, and it is important to note; that God needs man for this to happen. More importantly, he needs intercessors to stand before His divinity and annul a wicked decree. God heard the desire that Mordecai sent Esther. Immediately she gives out an order that every Jew in every in every land where her message is heard, is to fast without food or water for three days. They all began to fast without questioning or opposing the order, it was an instant response. Haman's hatred did not prevail against the people of God because they all joined together in action. The decree of hatred and death against the people of God was broken by the fasting and praying of a unified people. There is power in togetherness!

There is a lot that could be said about decrees that have been set by men who are full of evil and hatred. As another example, we have the decree signed by King Darius, who signed an edict sentencing anyone who would dare to worship any other god that was not him. Daniel resisted the decree and continued praying to his Lord. This law was also sealed with the king's signet ring: *"Now, O king, issue the decree and put it in writing so that it cannot be altered—in accordance with the laws of the Medes and Persians, which cannot be repealed." So King Darius put the decree in writing." Daniel 6:8-9*

The spirit of darkness knows that heads of nations have the power to implement rulings. Nevertheless, the people of God must understand that He has given His church His own seal of authority for the church to use in His name. To speak out His Word is to speak forth His very decrees. Concrete prayers done in unity and one accord are very decisive in overthrowing the enemy's evil plans.

In those days, anyone caught disobeying a royal decree was thrown alive into a pit where there were hungry lions waiting: *"A stone was brought and laid over the mouth of the den; and the king sealed it with his own signet ring and with the signet rings of his nobles, so that nothing would be changed in regard to Daniel." Daniel 6:17*

The king was actually placing his seal on the rock, at the entrance to the den, to give evidence that no one would dare to overstep his mandate. Moreover, while the decree was thus established, even so God worked supernaturally to close the lions' mouths, giving testimony of Himself. And Daniel was spared this cruel death. Evidently, He is the living God who has the last word. This is a vital example of how divine sovereignty disrupts human decrees.

The lion is similar to the spirit of vengeance who launches attacks with the purpose of tearing, destroying and killing the spiritual life of a faithful believer. **The anointing for courage and trust that was deposited in God, nullified the demons of revenge that were operating through the lions.**

Jesus Christ was sentenced to death by a Roman decree, but it was the treason of the religious Jews at the time that instigated it. Rome put a seal on His tomb to keep it from being opened. And just as it seemed that Daniel had been defeated, so it appeared that Christ had been crushed by the sentencing of hateful and revengeful hearts.

But God Himself tore the seal and brought back to life His Son, the Living God! The demons did not know that in this act of dying and being raised from the dead, the decrees that had been written against us were being annulled (See *Colossians 2:14*).

Everything that opposes us has its origin in the decrees that are against us. They are driven to counteract the truths that have been established by God. These stand before our paths like seemingly impenetrable walls, and seek to hinder His true plans. In verse 14 of Colossians in the Amplified Bible it reads: *"Having cancelled and blotted out and wiped away the handwriting of the note (bond) with its legal decrees and demands which was in force and stood against us (hostile to us). This [note with its regulations, decrees, and demands] He set aside and cleared completely out of our way by nailing it to [His] cross."*

WE ONLY NEED TO CONFESS THE WORD OUT LOUD!

God, in this hour, is raising up prophets that will declare a breaking off of the seals that appear impossible to crack. Jesus Christ died in order to annul the decree from the Garden of Eden that said: *"For the wages of sin is death... Romans 6:23* Jesus Christ has a signet which says: "I have annulled your death sentence. With my hands wounded at the cross, I nailed the decrees of hatred against you and your family, and I've made you free."

Crucify yourself with Christ and the devil will have no authority over your death decree!

Taking Back the Lost Authority

Throughout the pages of this book, we have been tracing back the history of hatred. Now we can compare this actual history with our present day reality. In these times, laws are enacted which place the Christians' faith at a real compromise. And no doubt, we will feel these pressures increasingly as time marches on. The primary purpose of the spirit of revenge against the chosen ones, (which is already operating in the world) is an attempt to completely destroy the trust in God and His Word. In second place, it seeks to seal people with a mark that identifies them with the ideology of the new world system. Faithful Christians already have the seal of God, which is the "guarantee," (God's spiritual pledge), that gives testimony to the spiritual world that these are the private property of the Savior.

Action is the visible manifestation of invisible faith.

If only there was faith to believe, the decrees made by perverse and unbelieving people would be broken by prayer! This is the time to use faith, the time to believe in the authority that God has given the church to tie, bind, unbind, root out, conquer, rise up and edify.

These days we are seeing enormous rifts between the races, due to many affronts that attempt at creating division, such as financial imbalances, deep roots of hatred and the uncontrollable desires for vengeance and deep resentment within many bitter hearts of unforgiveness. Satan has people he controls, placed in key positions in cities and nations around the world. There are thousands who travel and move daily from one continent to another, from one city to another. All this is a major contributing factor to instability, as well as imbalances in the local budgets of many nations.

Many people marry out of superficial convenience, and for this reason, there are more divorces on the increase. Things look bleak, and yet, we must not doubt nor despair because God also has His instruments of good will in important places and at precise times. For this reason, you must believe that God has specific plans to carry out in favor of His children. The faith of every man and woman of God must increase in order to take possession of the place and authority that He has provided for him or her.

The Anointing for Restitution

When Job prayed for his friends and humiliated himself before God demonstrating his righteousness, was when he was restituted and received a gold ring. Job 42:11 says: "*Then all his brothers and all his sisters and all who had known him before came to him, and they ate bread with him in his house; and they consoled him and comforted him for all the adversities that the Lord had brought on him. And each one gave him one piece of money, and each a ring of gold.*"

Ask for the blessing that Job received after being tested, and like him receive seven times more than what was taken away from you. The modern church is like Joseph, the dreamer. How often have you dreamed of doing great things for God so that His name will be glorified amongst the nations and unbelievers might believe? We must claim the relevant words that are in *Genesis 41:42: "Then Pharaoh took off his signet ring from his hand and put it on Joseph's hand, and clothed him in garments of fine linen and put the gold necklace around his neck."* This is your season! This is the church's season!

It is the time for the children of God to have the ring of authority returned to them. You need to pray that you will be placed in position in key places so that you will receive the blessings that the Lord has promised for your life. The fine garments given to Joseph represent his position of authority. Because he was in a high position, Joseph had the authority to determine Egypt's economy. It is of God that you should yearn for the great things assigned to you, and for this, you need to have the mind of a prince. The gold necklace signifies his rank as governor.

The Ring of Authority

"The King has the ring and He gives it to

whomever He wishes." Do not forget that the Heavenly Father has all dominion and He has given it to His Son, Jesus the Christ. Through Him, his children also receive that authority. The ring of authority is placed on the ones who return home as well as those who remained. In the parable of the prodigal son, Jesus explained that the younger son spent all of the inheritance received from his father. God wants to restore his "squandering children" to the inheritance that they have dispersed. As long as they do not come home, they will wander alone and aimlessly without a father, eating out of misery together with unclean spirits (the pigs). However, in spite of it, the Father is always waiting for each child to make the right choices that will lead him to be completely restored. When a child makes a decision to return, the first thing that the Father does after hugging him is to put a ring on him. This qualifies him as a prince.

You will never have sufficient authority if you are not under the Father's covering.

THIS IS THE TIME TO RETURN HOME; WHCH MEANS TO TAKE UP THE ORIGINAL POSITION.

God is calling for His children to take their authentic position of authority. The very best thing for the soul is to recognize that the Father is the giver of the spiritual garments, as well as the ring of authority. However, it is of extreme importance for you to be physically under spiritual, apostolic and prophetic authority.

10

THE HERODIAN LINEAGE

...the alliance with the Roman Empire

Flavius Josephus was a great Jewish historian, a Pharisee, and descendant of a family of priests. Through his written accounts, he gives us a clear picture of Israel's dark years from the reconstruction of the temple by Zerubbabel, (prophesied in the book of Zechariah) until the birth of Christ. According to Josephus, Herod the Great was an outstanding political and military leader. While his lineage was actually Idumaean, (from Bedouins in the desert and not Jews), his thought, culture and origin were most certainly Greek. For this reason, he can be more accurately described as a foreign king that ruled Judea during the time of the Roman oppression. He gravitated towards the side of the Romans, in character as well as ideology, for he was arrogant and forceful, which earned him the trust of the Romans and obtained their support in overthrowing the Jewish lineage from the Hashmonaim, direct descendants of the Maccabees. In the year 40 BC, he was able to obtain the title of King of Judea from Mark Anthony. He was characterized as a ruthless and coldblooded man, who had many of his own family members killed for no other reason than his fear of losing the power of the throne. According to the Gospels, Herod was still alive at the birth of Jesus. (4 BC)

The arrival of three wise men from ancient Persia, searching for the birth of a child and guided by a star, greatly perturbed Herod's heart. Faced with such a threat to his power, he gave orders to kill every male child of less than two years old, to assure that no one would be able to take the continuity of power away from him, or his descendants. The Gospels tell the story of how an angel visited Joseph and warned him to flee to Egypt and protect the Child from death. Then, after some years pass, again we read in *Matthew 2:19-20* that while in Egypt Joseph was told in a dream to return to Israel, for the one who had hunted the Child was dead. A few years later, we are told in *Matthew 2:19-20*, that while the family was in Egypt they are advised in a dream to return to Israel, for the one persecuting the child has died.

Even though Herod was not a descendant in direct lineage from Amalek's genealogy, he was a product of the desert and with a great deal of ambition. He was also very much like previous oppressive conquerors from Greece and Rome. He felt that he was in the midst of an everlasting and infallible dominion. Never the less, like every mortal being, he reached the hour of his death. In "King Herod the Great," Flavius Josephus gives the following historical account:

> Herod's illness became worse by the day, being punished by God for the crimes he had committed. A form of fire was slowly consuming him, which manifested not only with the searing pain upon contact, but in great internal anguish. He felt a vehement hunger and desire for food, which was impossible to appease. After his distemper seized upon his whole body, and greatly disordered all its parts in various symptoms; there were continuous pains in his colon, and dropsically turnouts about his feet, an inflammation of the abdomen, and a putrefaction of his privy member that produced worms. When sitting up breathing was difficult and was aggravated by his fetid breath. Finally, he suffered violent spasmodic convulsions on all his members. It was said by

those given over to the study of divine sciences and by diviners that this was the punishment of God for his many acts of wickedness. And yet, in spite of his grievous illness and the awful pains seemingly impossible for anyone to withstand, he hoped for a cure and would call for the physicians. He preceded the death of his son, Antipater, whom he gave orders to have slain. His kingdom, after being made king by the Romans, lasted thirty-seven years. He was a man of uncontrolled wrath who was inhumane to all, and belittled everything just and righteous.

HEROD THE GREAT, ALONG WITH HIS WHOLE LINEAGE, ARE SIMILAR TO THE FUTURE ANTICHRIST. THEY ARE CHARACTERIZED BY THE LIMITLESS AMBITION FOR POWER AND MURDER, BUT ESPECIALLY FOR THE PERSECUTION OF THE SAINTS, PROPHETS AND APOSTLES OF JESUS CHRIST.

Herod had many children by his ten wives, but he had three of them executed. During his time of great pain he designated one of his sons, Archelaus, as the successor to the throne. After his death, the emperor Tiberius Caesar divided the kingdom amongst his three sons. The author of the Gospel of Luke describes the events in chapter 3, verses 1 and 2, as follows: *Now in the fifteenth year of the reign of Tiberius Caesar, when Pontius Pilate was governor of Judea, and Herod was tetrarch of Galilee, and his brother Philip was tetrarch of the region of Ituraea and Trachonitis, and Lysanias was tetrarch of Abilene, n the high priesthood of Annas and Caiaphas, the word of God came to John, the son of Zacharias, in the wilderness.*

The word *tetrarch* means "a ruler." As we said before, Herod's three sons were governing three separate regions that were assigned directly from Rome. M Therefore, we read in *Mathew 2:22* how Joseph heard that Archelaus was ruling in place of his father Herod, and he was afraid to go back there. For this reason, he decided to go live in the region of Galilee, and specifically in a town called Nazareth.

Herod's Lineage

Herod Archelaus was very insecure and living with his brother Philip's wife. Herodias was clever and presumptuous, a reflection of Jezebel. Later on, he is affronted by the word of the prophet John the Baptist. Wanting to quell his conscience, he sent the prophet to prison. Out of revenge, Herodias asks her daughter to request for the head of the prophet from Herod.

Treacherous actions; lies, murder, were very common in the Roman Empire. These things were considered a normal part of life and were accepted by people of that time. Treason and vengeance were latent, and were always part of the background.

"The Herodian Lineage," is a symbol of the empires that will govern before the second coming of Christ. Just as murder and treason was the common denominator among the rulers in Herod's time, today murder, kidnappings, vengeance and hatred has expanded throughout all of the continents of the world.

The Herodians at the time of Christ were a religious sect that were opposed to Jesus Christ and were always trying to find fault in Him. *Mark 12:13* describes it as follows*: Then they sent some of the Pharisees and Herodians to Him in order to trap Him in a statement.* Jesus knew them well and often mentioned what they were really about, (see *Mathew 22:15-18, Mark 3:5-7*). Likewise, today's genuine Christian is attacked continually from every angle by those who are looking out for his faults, be they co-workers, family, friends or even strangers.

Herod represents all of the hatred that Haman had against the people of God, the abhorrence of Esau towards his brother, Korah's rebellion against the law of God, and the hatred of Islam against the nation of Israel and faithful Christians.

Herod persecuted the apostles. Luke writes in the book of *Acts 12:2-3: And he had James the brother of John put to death with a sword. When he saw that it pleased the Jews, he proceeded to arrest Peter ...]*

If we analyze the spirit with which Herod moved, we can see that the same spirit is working today. Herod represents all those who persecute the child and does not see the star, but inquires about it. In other words, people who have no prophetic revelation but seeks to know the future. The star represents the divine destiny chosen by God to lead His children into success, the place picked and prepared by the Creator. When the Magi from the orient visit Herod and ask about the promised Child King who is to be born, Herod immediately orders an investigation to find out in what city this is to take place. He cunningly asked the Magi in secret where the star appeared. (see *Matthew 2:7*) Naturally, Herod has absolutely no desires to recognize and worship the Child as King; rather, he wants to do away with him. He has no interest in prophecies; moreover, he wants to defend his position as dictator. In his natural strength, he would never yield his position to the true King, for he only wants veneration for himself. Herod is similar to all those that oppose Jesus Christ, they seek, but not because they are interested in the One truth, but because they secretly plan to destroy Him.

NOT EVERYTHING THAT GOD SHOWS YOU IS FOR YOU TO SHARE WITH THOSE WHO DO NOT HAVE THE SAME VISION AS YOU. OFTEN, GOD SHOWS YOU THINGS SO THAT YOU CAN PRAY IN LINE WITH HIS PLANS.

As soon as a star announces the birth of a prophet, Herod and his kingdom get set on alert. Why? In order to ensnare, confine and make sure he never reaches the destiny preset by God. The goal of the Herodian spirit is to make the person wander aimlessly and never reach his destination. Just how many, we ask ourselves, are lost within strange doctrines and errors where they will never be truly useful in the hands of God?

Herod is a Destructor Who Changes Destinies

Herod's victims become wandering stars, without divine destiny or plans. They never reach the goal. (see *Judas 13*)

The Bible says, *"there are eunuchs who were made eunuchs by men,"* (see *Matthew 19:12*) spiritually castrated and sterile. Herod is a spirit connected to envy and hatred and does not want to see anyone obtain God's blessings. Sometimes he achieves his purpose. How? By assigning persons or agents of destruction to young people, making them fall into diverse sins, drugs, addictions, pornography, etc. He is always behind adultery in a marriage causing spouses to separate. To local churches he sends Salome, Herodias, Dalila or Jezebel to cut the heads off of true prophets. To able businessmen, he tempts into dishonorable alliances so that they will end up bankrupt and unable to contribute to divine plans.

Many ministries and Christian businesses are being thus attacked by hateful and envious individuals, who like demonic spies, infiltrate key places.

When you constantly dedicate your life, finances, and ministry into the hands of Almighty God, you will soon discover the spirit of the Herodians.

What was the intention of the Herodian lineage? To kill the true King. In our present day, we see this manifested in revengeful and degrading desires. This spirit attempts against the Godly projects and visions of faithful believers. It tries to amputate divine purposes before they have even been announced.

Alliances with the Roman Empire

The alliances that Herod made with the Roman Empire gave him greater power and authority, for him as well as his descendants. Keep in mind that the world system, or the NOW (New World Order) that will rise up against humanity and especially Christians, will be formed by unions and alliances. This is how it will gain the strength to rule the world. The *Dragon*, the ancient serpent Satan, will give power to the beast, for the great world system. (see *Revelations 12*)

The beast that the apostle John saw in a vision had seven heads and ten horns. In *Revelations 12*, it speaks of a system (the beast) with seven heads and ten horns, (who are the leaders or presidents that will be in place at the time as the "great elite," or the ten regions in which the world is divided by financial regions. There will be an alliance among them, although we must remember that in the book of Daniel, the kingdoms on earth through the ages are symbolized by a statue. This statue composed of layers of elements representing each successive age, had iron and clay at its feet. This shows that this world alliance was be a complete sham, as iron and clay can never truly mix. Therefore, the feet of the statue, meaning the support of all the world's systems, was constructed of an unsound mixture of elements and will not stand.

"And in that you saw the iron mixed with common clay, they will combine with one another in the seed of men; but they will not adhere to one another, even as

iron does not combine with pottery [...] Inasmuch as you saw that a stone was cut out of the mountain without hands and that it crushed the iron, the bronze, the clay, the silver and the gold, the great God has made known to the king what will take place in the future; so the dream is true and its interpretation is trustworthy." Daniel 2:43, 45

The Roman Empire, as crude iron, represents the legs of these earthly kingdoms, but just as feet have ten toes, in the same way the ten "horns" are the leaders of the nations.

What Does the Beast Represent?

Their unity is the alliances that the rulers of great world powers have formed.

The characteristics of this beast are similar to what Daniel mentions in his book (see *Daniel 7*). There is a similarity. The prophet was able to see one of the ten horns that had eyes and a mouth and was speaking "great things." However, his language was against the Almighty God and his saints, words of blasphemy and hate. If the beast (NOW) has seven heads, one of the horns will be the one who will speak for the entire world system, and we have no doubt this will be the Antichrist.

Now we have looked at how inside the Roman Empire, the senate and all allied subjects operated under the same spirit. This was the same spirit that was working in Herod and which he passed to his descendants. For these and many other reasons, there is an accurate comparison between Herod's lineage and those who will be the heads of nations in the near future. In the same manner, they will come together in the one same mind and one same ideology as the leader of the great one world system. The apostle John in his letter wrote that this system is already at work unseen.

THERE IS AN URGENT LAST DAY CALL TO HIS CHURCH, TO SEEK MORE OF HIM AND TO STAND IN POSITION TO RECEIVE HIS PROMISED BLESSINGS!

You will read of this and more in the next chapter.

11

FROM SERPENT TO DRAGON

...from the beginning to the end of time

We have been looking at how an unhealed wound in the heart gives place to anger, which gives place to resentment and ultimately runs from generation to generation throughout the ages. We could conclude, therefore, that when resentment entrenches itself within the heart and it is not taken out in time, it could lead into disastrous thoughts of revenge.

VENGEANCE IS REALLY NO LESS THAN WANTING TO SEE THE PRESUMED ENEMY CRUSHED OR DEAD.

Sometimes, resentment proceeds from a familiar spirit that is able to influence others, as long as all share common ideas.

We have also seen how this condition began as an

insignificant envy in the heart of Cain, which led him to the extreme dishonor of being known as the first murderer in human history.

Let's review the process: What started in the heart of Cain, grew like snake venom that had a direct effect in Amalek's grandchild. It continued down the Amalkite's descendants until it reached the blood of King Agag. It continued its course into Persia through Haman and spread and spread all along the trajectory of history. It manifested in individuals like King of Tirus, Nebuchadnezzar, Antioch IV, Herod the Great, Napoleon Bonaparte, Hitler and many others. They all had something in common: to go against the object of their hatred, the genuine seed of God.

The Ancient Serpent in the Garden of Eden

It is known that in Eden, Satan used the serpent and entered in it to speak to Eve, seducing and deceiving her. In Revelations it is named as the "ancient serpent," but at the end of ages, it is called "the great dragon." *Revelations 12:9*

The dragon is Satan, the ancient serpent, father of

lies, deceit and hatred. Satan appeared to humans for only three purposes: to kill, to steal and to destroy. *Vengeance brings with it the desire to kill and destroy.* At other times, Satan is compared to a flying serpent, mentioned in *Isaiah 14:29- 27:1.*

The flying spirit represents demonic control over the air and the minds that it wants to influence. Identified as the one who operates over the children of disobedience in *Ephesians 2:2,* this spirit was defeated by Esther, Moses, the prophet Samuel, and of course, Jesus Christ Himself.

The Fall of the Dragon

1. *"I have cast you as profane from the mountain of God." Ezekiel 28:16* Satan was cast out from the mountain of God because he was full of "violence," a word which comes from the Hebrew *kjamas,* a primitive root which means "injustice, unjustly, cruel, aggravating, false, injurious, evil, iniquitous". To cast out, or to expel, comes from the Hebrew "kjalal," a primitive root meaning: "to profane, dishonor, humiliate, stain, wound, kill".

2. *"I was watching Satan fall from heaven like lightning." Luke 10:18* Jesus says that He saw

him fall like lighting. In *Isaiah 14:12* it recounts that he would "weaken" nations. The word "weaken" comes from the Hebrew *kjalash*, which is to "thrash down, overthrow, to decay, to vanish". Later, in verse 13 he says: "*I will ascend*," from the Hebrew *rum*, which means, "exalt, fill with pride, arrogance, lofty, overbearing, over proud."

3. *"I will cast you to the ground."* Ezekiel 28:17 (also see *Isaiah 14:12*). Satan exalted himself, from the Hebrew *gabaj*, which means "arrogant, proud, lofty, to become haughty, to become vain". He also became corrupt, from *shakjat*, which is "to corrupt, destroy, devastate, squander, destroy, hurt, kill, lie in waiting, spoil, ruin, damage, demolish, depraved".

4. *"And he threw him into the abyss […] so that he would not deceive the nations any longer."* "Deceive," from the Greek *planao*, which means "to wander" (away from security, truth or virtue) deceiver, lie, erratic, lose, lead astray, seduce."

5. *"Nevertheless you will be thrust down to Sheol, to the recesses of the pit."* Isaiah 14:15

6. *"And the devil who deceived them was thrown into the lake of fire and brimstone…*

Revelations 20:12

How do You Win the War Against Amalek?

In the first place, let's take a look at how Amalek was defeated. It was actually done by working in unity in a team effort. As you can see, unison is a very powerful weapon! Sometimes battles are lost because of divided mindsets. Therefore, work teams must come together and unite to form a common front. Achieving consensus is one of the best strategies in order to overcome all opposition. *Matthew 18:19* says: *"Again I say to you, that if two of you agree on earth about anything that they may ask, it shall be done for them by My Father who is in heaven."*

The act of coming into agreement works to give good results in any area. One example of this is in marriage, where apart from love, the most powerful quality a couple can possess is the ability to communicate openly and in mutual trust. Another example of agreement is between a pastor and his ministry team.

If in the leadership ranks, there is a person who

thinks differently from the vision that God has given the pastor, that will be a major obstacle for receiving the blessing for the area in which they are working. Consequently, to come into agreement and of one accord is not only effective in Christian circles, but is an ancient strategy that will always work when it is applied.

The tower of Babel is an example of single-mindedness. (See *Genesis 11*) They got together for a specific purpose and they would have achieved it if God had not intervened in time. They were getting very far, and that would have been very dangerous for the earth and the plans that God wanted to bring to pass on behalf of His people.

Thus, it is evident that in the past as well as in present times, powerful alliances have formed that have met their purpose, whether these be for good or for evil. The secret to achieving a targeted goal is to work as a team and being of like mind.

Although there are many congregations that claim to represent the true church of Jesus Christ on earth, these are often subject to divisions and give an image before the entire world of incompatibility, instability and over all, a bad example.

Hence, Amalek is defeated by believing and acting out in unity, while recognizing that a team is more powerful than a single individual. In true unity, the concepts of supremacy and self-importance are lost. God is no respecter of persons, therefore we can conclude that in His eyes we are all equal, simply that some have been given more responsibilities than others.

King Davis is a relevant example of teamwork within the context of a Messianic Kingdom. Upon analyzing his court, we see that David had:

- Princes
- Army Generals
- Chancellor
- Priests
- Personal Secretary (Savsa)
- The Prophet Nathan
- Advisors
- The brave were his right hand

In those days there were in Israel one million, one hundred thousand that drew the sword, and in Judah four hundred, seventy thousand (see *1*

Chronicles 21:5).

In the Kingdom governance there are many functions, and they are differentiated only by the level of responsibility of each. There are the warriors, prophets, priests, subjects, sons, chancellors, secretaries, treasurers, etc. If they can all work together with the same frame of mind, then they can put the most perfect plan to fruition, which is to live in peace and harmony.

Another method of overcoming Amalek is dying to the personal will - the SELF. We need to strive to practice Jesus' prayer before dying: *"Father, that they may be one, even as You and I are One"* (see *John 17*). This is the wisest petition anyone has ever asked. Jesus uttered this before reaching His primary purpose for which He had voluntarily given Himself: *"that they may all be one; even as You, Father, are in Me and I in You, that they also may be in Us, so that the world may believe that You sent Me"* *John 17:21*

The Church, as an assembly, comes together in unity because it is in Jesus and Jesus is in the Father. The Father, Jesus Christ and the Holy Spirit have always worked as a team, the three that are one have always existed, they have the same mind, have never divided, have remained this way eternally and will be so forever. This is the reason His name is YHVH (Jehovah), which means "to be," "the one who exists within Himself". This is the best example of overcoming as a team.

How do You Win the War Against Agag?

With the anointing of prophetic establishment. Samuel represents the restored glory and the holy, whole, transparent, and genuine priesthood. The truth and the covering defeat hatred, by the power of God. The prophetic anointing is as important these days as pastoral ministry.

A prophet is not just one who prophesies inspired by the Holy Spirit, but also one who implements and establishes the righteousness of God. His actions give testimony to the truth and are backed by the presence of God. Samuel did not walk trying to please everyone, but rather he would testify from the word that he would hear from God. Samuel knew that God's will was to finish off His enemies, because to not do so would mean they would rise in greater power in the following generation. Agag is overcome by divine justice flowing from the hand of a righteous man who knows how to hear and obey His voice. Saul would allow feelings to lead him. God's servants cannot be subject to feelings and emotions. On the contrary, they should be alert and be led by the Holy Spirit while covering their minds so as not to fall into the traps of the enemy. Samuel judged as a prophet and priest before God.

SAMUEL ALSO REPRESENTS THE INTERCESSION AND THE ALTAR THAT PROPHETS RAISE DAILY. HEREIN LIES TRUE BALANCE AGAINST DECEIT AND FALSEHOOD.

"Let the priests, the Lord's ministers, Weep between the porch and the altar, And let them say, Spare Your people, Oh Lord..." Joel 2:17

When ministers and servants of the Lord cry out to detain the forces of hate and evil and even God's own judgment because of sin, heaven opens its doors. Persecution rises up against the righteous and the congregation of saints, not against those who have formed alliances of evil and conspiracies to deceive and swindle the innocent. For it is the saints that testify of the truth with their lives. Unity and one accord in prayer is vital in the midst of crisis, despair, famine and even plagues.

IN ORDER TO RECEIVE THE PRECISE ANSWERS FOR PRESSING NEEDS IN THESE UNCERTAIN TIMES, IT IS NECESSARY TO PRAY PRAYERS OF AGREEMENT.

The Bible says: *"Keep watching and praying that you may not enter into temptation"* (*Matthew 26:41*) The word "temptation" here refers to *peirasmos*, which means "to be put into trial by means of good or evil, in the midst of adversity."

It is as if you were told: "Do not fall asleep spiritually, better yet, keep your eyes wide open and do not cease to pray. See that you do not enter into trials nor give in to evil, but remain free that you may be delivered from adversities"

How do You Win the War Against Haman?

Three days of fasting by an entire nation of believers overcame an order sealed by the king.

Haman was sentenced with the same weapon that he used himself. The death trap that he prepared for Mordecai, was instead used for him and his offspring.

There was a planned genocide of enormous proportions for all of the Jewish people living under the regime of the Persian Empire. Mordecai joined his heart to Esther's and was able to implement a powerful strategy of uniting the entire Jewish population in a fast of no food or water for three days.

And then, in a marvelous turn of events and through divine intervention, the law that had distilled death did not prevail over God's chosen people.

FASTING, TOGETHER WITH CRYING OUT TO GOD, WAS THE MOST POWERFUL WEAPON THEY USED TO SAVE THEIR LIVES FROM CERTAIN DEATH.

Learn from this practical example; hatred can certainly be overcome!

How do You Win the War Against Herod?

Sending confusion to the enemy on God's behalf and His divine justice. The Word of God says that Herod became confused. Just as Joseph, Mary's husband, also became confused, yet the Angel of the Lord appeared to him in dreams to bring him peace and remind him that what he was doing was right and the work of God. Although at that pointing time, Joseph did not understand, he trusted that God was in complete control of the situation. He received comfort and direction regarding Mary, but he especially learned to believe and trust completely in his God.

WE DO NOT ALWAYS UNDERSTAND THE ENTIRE PICTURE, BUT ONE THING WE HAVE TO KNOW FOR SURE, THAT IF GOD IS IN THE MATTER WE SHOULD TRUST AND GO FORTH.

How Will We Win the War Against the Antichrist and the World System?

An example from Korah's rebellion. We can gain

insight for this by meditating on the example of the rebellion of Korah against Moses and the punishment given by God Himself. Just as God dealt in the desert with Korah, Datan and Abiram (see *Psalm 106:16*) and all of their families for uniting to run contrary to the Word of God given to Moses. These three formed an alliance against the very will of God and His prophet. These alliances in opposition to God's divine precepts are so strong, that no one can take vengeance against them, only the Lord.

Korah and Abiram represent the rebellion against the law and order established by God on earth. This is the same type of punishment that the system of world control will receive at the end of the age. The principality that evolved throughout the ages until becoming the dragon, is the one that will give all of its power to the "beast," and it is composed of hatred, haughtiness and thirst for vengeance.

In the end, the very presence of God will overcome. Today, this beast is hidden behind terrorism, organized crime, racial hatred, assassinations, fanatical religious cults, and manifests in the cold indifference towards human misery. The vision given to the apostle John announces that in the end, it will be swallowed by the earth and sent alive to Sheol. Very similar to the end of Korah's rebellion.

History repeats itself again and the cycle begins once more. In *Revelations 12* it says that Satan (the dragon) will give all of its power to the "beast". This is a figurative name given to the political, financial and social union constituting the system that will govern the world. It will be presided by a man operating under the complete influence of the spirit of iniquity, and will be called "the man of sin". He will institute the most horrible persecution of hatred against the saints in history. However, this will be a brief period of time that will be allowed by God.

All of these things that will take place will not be carried out by one man alone, but with the collaboration of many others who will in turn represent their respective regions on earth. They will of course be acting in complete agreement and single purpose, (and after a number of wars to bring dissident countries into submission). This act on the part of the dragon (Satan) to give all of his power to the new world order system, will be similar to the bestowing of a ring of authority to each one of the leaders of the ten heads. Since there is a horn that stands out from the other horns and has eyes and a mouth (see *Daniel 7:8*), we can surmise that this will be no other than the voice of the dragon speaking directly to the world.

The apostle John says: *"This is the spirit of the antichrist, of which you have heard that it is coming, and now it is already in the world." 1 John 4:3-4*

In *2 Thessalonians 2:22*, he is called in the following manner: "the son of perdition"

The Brief Persecution

Hate has appeared time and again all throughout history, manifested by persons with different names, one common spirit. The name this man has now we do not know, what we do know is that he will rise up with the same spirit that these men had, but with much greater delegated power and authority to persecute everything that emanates from God and His Christ.

It doesn't matter what his name is going to be, what is truly important is the work that he will accomplish by means of unbelievable supernatural power, such as has never been seen.

In Daniel he is mentioned as the horn that rises and stands out, moved by a spirit of malevolent ambition and avarice. With long-standing decrees against God's remnant, he will persecute those who have remained on earth.

This period of time will be brief, but its beginning and end will be exclusively at the hands of the Sovereign God. None of what will take place will be at the hands of the heathen, nor will it be within the scope of their decisions. The Lord Himself will permit it and the prophets have already written what is to come.

The Word of God says that nothing occurs without the Lord revealing it to his servants and prophets. *Does a lion roar in the thicket when he has no prey? Does he growl in his den when he has caught nothing? Does a bird fall into a trap on the ground where no snare has been set? Does a trap spring up from the earth when there is nothing to catch? When a trumpet sounds in a city, do not the people tremble? When disaster comes to a city, has not the Lord caused it? Surely the Sovereign Lord does nothing without revealing his plan to his servants the prophets. The lion has roared — who will not fear? The Sovereign Lord has spoken — who can but prophesy? Amos 3:4-8*

In our day, the Church is on earth and is its salt and light, and her mission is to preserve the nations from the threat of evil. Isaiah speaks of how "darkness will cover the earth," but also gives a promise regarding the chosen remnant: *"thick darkness is over the peoples, but the Lord rises upon you and his glory appears over you" Isaiah 60:2*

The Church is militant and is holding back wickedness, because she has been given the authority in the name of Jesus Christ to do so... *"and the gates of Hades* (the empire of death) *will not overcome it."* (*Matthew 16:18*) The word "overcome" in Greek *katisju*, means "to conquer, surpass, defeat." We need to understand that as long as the Church is waging war over the earth, the empire of death will not be able to vanquish her. Once the Church is removed from earth, men will be left in total darkness.

GOD HAS GIVEN POWER TO THE CHURCH TO CONQUER OVER EVIL, BUT

TODAY, LESS THAN FIFTY PERCENT OF CHRISTIANS KNOW HOW TO MAKE FULL USE OF THIS POWER DELEGATED BY GOD OVER THEIR LIVES.

The goal of the New World Order will be to reduce the numbers of population (regardless of ethnicities, children, families, etc). This system will try by all means possible to fulfill its gruesome covenants. Yet, in spite of this goal, there will be many who will be saved by giving their lives because of their faith. *Revelations 7:13-14* makes reference of them when it says: *"These who are clothed in the white robes, who are they, and where have they come from?" I said to him, "My lord, you know." And he said to me, "These are the ones who come out of the great tribulation, and they have washed their robes and made them white in the blood of the Lamb"*.

The Holy Spirit is on the Church's Side

There is a promise on *2 Thessalonians 2:7* that fills us with hope: *"For the mystery of lawlessness is already at work; only he who now restrains will do so until he is taken out of the way."*

From this text we glean that from the very first time that Jesus ascended into heaven, vengeance began to be loosed upon the earth against faithful Christians. Furthermore, we see that full hatred towards God's saints is being held back from fully manifesting.

The only one who is able to bring about such an immense task of impediment, is the Holy Spirit. So long as He remains residing in the Church, which is His temple, the barrier to the man of sin will continue and he will not be apparent. Only after the removal of the Church, will this ministry of impediment cease, then iniquity will reach its pinnacle and the antichrist will be revealed.

At that point, "hate incarnate" will be fully unleashed over the whole earth. In this same text in 2 Thessalonians we are told in the manner that this mystery of lawlessness works. Different translations refer to him as "always working undercover," meaning, he has always existed, but has never been able to fully manifest.

Without a doubt, God is the only one who will give the order when the precise time comes, of removing that which up until the present was holding him up. We fully understand that there is someone who is standing and restraining something that wants to get through. The spirit of hatred and vengeance has been continually moving "under cover". Notwithstanding, all throughout time, God always raises up those who win battles by their prayers and faith. God wants to make you more than a conqueror in the place that He has put you. He is with you when you battle in your church, serving as the body of Christ.

Each Must Win Their Own Battles

The great war of the ages and the establishment of the Kingdom of God on earth, belong only to God the Creator and Almighty King, Jesus Christ. He is the winner and will do so through His supernatural power. This is a war between hate and love, between arrogance and humility, between lofty hearts and contrite hearts. Winning a battle is not winning the war. This is why you must be an overcomer "in your own battles". You need to keep in mind that for every spirit of hatred and division that raises up against you, if you are a believer, you will succeed. Just as Joshua and the leader and intercessor Moses, Aaron and Esther and the entire multitude of people that fasted and prayed succeeded, you too will overcome and be victorious.

Jesus Christ Already Won the War

Jesus on the cross of Calvary has already won the war, and in His time, when the Father so establishes it, He will be honored by all of the nations on earth:

"Judah also will fight at Jerusalem; and the wealth of all the surrounding nations will be gathered, gold and silver and garments in great abundance. So also like this plague will be the plague on the horse, the mule, the camel, the donkey and all the cattle that will be in those camps. Then it will come about that any who are left of all the nations that went against Jerusalem will go up from year to year to worship the King, the Lord of hosts, and to celebrate the Feast of Tabernacles." Zacharias 14:14-16

Many prophetic texts tell us of the nations around the world that will bring their riches to honor the King.

Only Jesus Christ is the overcomer.

Who will be able to steal the glory from the only One who deserves it? All the Church can do is to receive the benefits of Calvary, and for this, she has salvation and is triumphant. Without Christ, she cannot prevail, for we owe everything to Him.

Within the framework of eternity, He will be the only conqueror. Those who followed Him until the end and the martyrs for His cause will reign with Him. Those who are worthy to sit on the thrones will judge the nations, because all of the triumph belongs to the Christ of glory.

Why should we believe that the Church is helping to establish the Kingdom, when the Father has only given Him all dominion, glory and power? Only before Him will every knee bow. The Bible prophecies emphasize the splendor of His coming and the sword in His mouth with which He will destroy His enemies, and with this, He will give evidence that He does not fight, because He is ALREADY A WINNER.

Jesus Christ defeated His enemies on the cross of Calvary, and now, on His second coming He will only return to take up His Kingdom. The Kingdom is not taken by the Church because the Father has

211

already given it to Jesus. The Father will also give Him the power to reign on earth because He has overcome.

The Church does not play the leading role in this, because God the Father made the entire center of the universe to be only for Him.

JESUS CHRIST IS THE ONE WHO DIED AND ROSE AGAIN AND IS SEATED AT THE RIGHT HAND OF GOD. HE WILL RETURN AS THE OVERCOMER. BY FAITH IN HIM, THE CHURCH RECEIVES THE POWER TO BE PARTAKERS OF THE INHERITANCE IN CHRIST AND TO REIGN WITH HIM.

TO HIM BE ALL OF THE GLORY FOREVER AND EVER!

12

FREEDOM FROM RESENTMENTS!

Anger, One Step to Resentment

We want to briefly resume the following: Unquestionably, anger is a very dangerous emotion, and if taken to extremes, it can become a grudge that is carried over into wrath. Generally, this strong emotion is accompanied by discomfort, bitterness and indignation. No doubt, the causes are always injustices or offenses that grow inside the heart, however, these catalysts can be very real and cause much inner pain, but they can also be fantasies, products of the imagination.

The consequences of living under this type of emotional pressures can be as dangerous as a time bomb. In the long run, it can cause physical problems so serious to the point that the person becomes gradually ill without even realizing it. These negative emotions cause chemical imbalances that are damaging throughout the body; headaches, migraines, heart attacks and bleeding ulcers are just a few examples.

Resentment grows out of frustration. This is the first sign that a person is struggling with feelings of hostility. Generally, it grows to the same degree as the inability of the individual to achieve the plans laid out in his heart and mind. Often, those plans and goals do not come from God. Quite often, they are ideas stemming from the pressures of living in a competitive society. Having goals is very important, but not all goals are achievable.

With the passing of time, frustrations can grow so large that any spark can provoke a major explosion, in addition, the person will feel guilty inside for not being able to live up to expectations. This makes the growing resentment to focus on the person or situation that the individual feels stood in the way of his success.

Resentment is one of the primary ingredients in feelings of guilt. People who bear grudges feel guilty and irate. There are many individuals who spend a great deal of their lifetimes struggling against these feelings.

Not being able to forget what someone did to them in the past, makes that person a slave to the situation, leaving an open, unhealed wound. The worst part is, that every time the thought comes up, the feelings attached are just as strong as if the assault had just happened.

To get rid of anger is the very best decision that a person can make. On the cross, Jesus pardoned those who were despising and reviling Him. He asked His Father to forgive them and not take their actions into consideration. However, Jesus was not only pardoning His attackers, He was pardoning you and me as well.

How Do You Get Rid of Anger?

Only you, with the aid of the Holy Spirit can accomplish that. How? Recognizing first of all, that the fault lies in you and not others. Secondly, forgiving yourself and forgiving God. Is it possible that God needs you to forgive Him? Of course not! You are the one who needs to be free.

STOP LOOKING FOR OTHERS TO BLAME AND ACKNOWLEDGE THAT WHAT YOU REALLY NEED IS GOD'S FORGIVENESS.

Replace your resentments for obedience to the Word of God, and frustrations for the joy of the Lord. The Holy Spirit is wonderful! Allow faith and joy to substitute your guilt and resentment. These things will effectively help you to feel differently.

Joy will fill your soul when you stop demanding yourself for answers to questions such as: "Why has this happened to me?" Stop looking for guilt and pointing fingers! Don't be a victim! Stop focusing on the problem and instead extend your vision forward saying to yourself: *"Yes, I can!" "Yes, I will be able to exchange resentment for love!"* When you stop accusing yourself and others, you will begin to trust in yourself and others, a new light will appear in your shadows. The situation will take a dramatic turn.

RENOUNCE RESENTMENT AND UNFORGIVENESS. FORGIVE YOURSELF. CAST ASIDE THE DESIRE TO CONTROL EVERYTHING.

Allow the Holy Spirit to be your teacher! Let go of self-reliance and believe God with all of your heart. God is perfect, good and just. Human beings make mistakes, not God. Don't forget that Jesus, through His faithful Spirit, helps us out of our mistakes. Don't allow your mind to continue being a ground for accusations from the enemy!

Never again, allow anger and resentment to remain lodged in your heart. If you learn to overcome within you, your future generations will be able to do the same. No matter how tough things have been for you in life, keep in mind that Jesus has already paid for it.

Love Vs. Hate

Jesus Christ is love in essence, not in words. He became love and took on the body of a man to save us. Love is the opposite of rejection. Rejection is an attitude of loveless contempt towards another. Society as a whole is bombarded by rejection.

The love of God is a subject matter that receives far little attention from pulpits and is not practiced enough. What is needed is a baptism (immersion) of love that will set lives completely free from old grudges and suppressed anger. The world speaks of "love," but this is only an act of selfishness, of wanting to have for one's own ends. In this manner, saying "I love you" is only an expression used to channel selfish desires, a craving to receive but not share. However, true love is an act of devotion to others, has no limits, is not selfish, and does not hold RESENTMENTS.

Here is the secret: for you who have faithfully followed this book page after page until the end. The answer is: YES!!, hatred and resentment can be demolished and the weapon of war is the genuine love of God. To love even those who have hurt us, not wanting to return evil for evil, instead, return good for evil...It might seem like we are speaking in a strange language from another galaxy. Nevertheless, more than a feeling or simple words, this is the action that we must practice: *agape* love.

God is infinite, He has no beginning and no end, this is a mystery that is difficult to understand. So are His ways. It is very easy to say "I love my wife" or "I love my husband," especially when on a honeymoon, but although this *eros* love is given by God, it is entirely different.

But the true test of love is found in our response to others, towards those who use us, mock us, that hate us and try to blackmail and betray us. These are the situations where the only thing that will do is the manifest love of God, the real **agape**. *"Examine me, Oh Lord, and try me; Test my mind and my heart."* (Psalm 26:2)

Prayer of Release:

I will invoke my Lord in prayer and through His forgiveness I will be saved from my enemies. Today, I am willing to forgive those who hurt me in my past. I will no longer judge their hearts because now II rest in the righteousness of God. I give up forever the darkness of my past, so that I may live in the light of a new and triumphant day that the Lord has prepared for me. Today I will be like a sheep taken into the hands of the Good Shepherd. I believe that He will anoint my head with oil and I will be whole.

I understand, that if I do not forgive I will continue to be a slave to my feelings of hatred and anger, that affect my life and the life of those that I love. Examine my painful memories, repressed and hidden down in the bottom of my heart. I renounce making my heart a cave of Edom, holding grudges in darkness. You are my Lord, and in You I trust.

God and Heavenly Father, today I cry out to you so that You will free me through forgiveness. I acknowledge before You that in my own human strength it is impossible for me to forgive, because there is anger, hate, impotence, and frustrations plaguing my soul. And yet, today I have made a decision to be free, and I surrender into Your hands my painful memories, and the people who hurt me. I forgive them just as You have forgiven me.

Right now I release every desire for vengeance. I give You every single burden that have been able to oppress my life.

You where the One who formed my body, soul and spirit, this is why I know that You can heal my soul where my negative emotions and destructive desires reside. I can be free of resentments and anger. I know they hurt me, but I also hurt others. Thank You Lord, because You have forgiven me.

You tell me in Your Word that it is necessary to forgive seventy times seven, and now I understand that this means always having to forgive in order to live free. Today I want to forgive from my past, up until this day and forever. I declare that I am free of every oppression and the chains that were binding me.

Lord, today I make the best and greatest decision of my life in pardoning to be permanently free. Thank You that You saw me in your love, and are breaking and removing hatred from me forever. I know that others hurt me because they too, had wounds in their own hearts. Today is the day that I choose to forgive them and the chains of hatred, resentment and vengeance will no longer have me as a slave.

I forgive my parents, I forgive them in the name of Jesus, and I give You thanks, Lord, because now I know that I was not born by accident or chance, but because You wanted me to come to this world. I know that You always loved me eternally, and so now I forgive my parents.

I forgive my earthly father, who was absent during my childhood. My father who hurt me, mistreated and abused me. I forgive him because only you know of his wounded heart Many hurts filled his heart with anger and hatred, and that is why he didn't know how to love me. I now fully forgive my earthly father and I'm free of the bad memories of him.

I now forgive my mother for having rejected me, for having tried to get rid of me while I was still in her womb. I forgive my mother and I let go of the pain she has caused me and of every destructive judgment I have raised against her.

I give You thanks, Lord, because it was already written that I would come into this world. I also give You thanks for having protected my life. Thank You for Your Word that declares: *"So do not fear, for I am with you; do not be dismayed, for I am your God. I will strengthen you and help you; I will uphold you with my righteous right hand."* Isaiah 41:10

Lord, I now forgive those who raised me when I was a child. My relatives and other persons who took care of me when I was unable to fend for myself. I forgive their lack of love, their absences, their lack of understanding, their inability to give a hug when I needed one. I forgive their physical violence and shouts that terrorized me. I now forgive them Lord, because now I know that they did not know Your wisdom or true love, the love that comes from God.

I forgive those who planted the seeds of hate in me through their acts of violence and aggression. I forgive them because they never knew Your genuine, authentic love.

Now I am free. I am free of being afraid of a god created in my imagination; a god bringing punishment for my sins because he was the god that I imagined in my childhood while I still did not know of Your Word and perfect love. Now I know that Yu are a God of forgiveness and mercy and I give You thanks because I know that You are my real God, and You bring peace to my heart.

I now forgive my partner who did not know how to love me and I forgive myself. I also forgive the person You bring to my heart and mind and place them in my thoughts before Your presence...

I now forgive all those who hurt and wounded me in any way. From today on, I will never permit hate and frustration to lead me into defeat. Right now I confess that I am free of the fear of failure.

I forgive because forgiveness frees me of guilt, of

anger, resentment, frustration, fear and everything that was tying me in the past. I forgive because through forgiveness I can walk free of the burdens of yesterday, always looking ahead in faith believing that I have a new life. Thank You Lord, because I know that You will continue to work with Your Holy Spirit in me, healing all my painful memories. I will not turn to look back at the darkness of the past, because You have cleansed me.

Thank You for the healing in my heart and because You have broken the shackles of my bondage in the world of darkness. Now I am in Your light... and You are the Light of the world. I declare and determine, in the all powerful name of Jesus Christ, that I am free forever of the spirit of hatred. I declare that he no longer has a place in my life nor in my family. I believe that I am positioned in a new level of blessings and victories, and that I will proclaim everywhere of the freedom that only Jesus Christ can give. In Jesus' name, Amen!

BIBLIOGRAPHY

Rainbow Study Bible - Reina-Valera 1960, (Spanish Edition) Broadman & Holman, Nashville, TN, 1995

Biblia Plenitud (Spirit-Filled Life Bible-Spanish Edition) Jack W. Hayford, editor, Reina-Valera 1960, Editorial Caribe Nashville, TNN, 1994

Strong's New Exhaustive Bible Concordance, (Spanish Edition) James Strong, Editorial Caribe, Miami, FL 2002

Vine's Complete Expository Dictionary of Old and New Testament Words, (Spanish Edition) W.E. Vine, Editorial Caribe, Nashville, TN, 1999

MacArthur Study Bible (Spanish Edition) John MacArthur, Editorial Portavoz, Grand Rapids, MI, 2005

Wikipedia, The Free Encyclopedia, registered trademark of Wikipedia Foundation, updated July 22, 2004 http:en.wikipedia.org/wiki/Main_Page.

New American Standard Bible - Reference Edition(English Edition) Collins World, The Lockman Foundation, La Habra, CA 1975

www.ingramcontent.com/pod-product-compliance
Lightning Source LLC
Chambersburg PA
CBHW061017280326
41935CB00009B/997